Exorcising Preaching

Crafting Intellectually Honest Worship

Exorcising & Preaching

Crafting Intellectually Honest Worship

Nathan C. Walker

CHALICE
PRESS
ST. LOUIS, MISSOURI

Cover art: Shutterstock.com

www.ChalicePress.com

Print: 9780827208445   EPUB: 9780827208452   EPDF: 9780827208469

Library of Congress Cataloging-in-Publication Data

Walker, Nathan C., 1975-
    Exorcising preaching : crafting intellectually honest worship / Nathan
        C. Walker.
        pages cm
    Includes bibliographical references and index.
    ISBN 978-0-8272-0844-5 (pbk. : alk. paper)
    1. Preaching. 2. Unitarian Universalist Association. I. Title.
    BV4211.3.W345 2014
    251—dc23
                            201403625

Contents

*Dedicated to the members and friends of the
First Unitarian Church of Philadelphia,
a Unitarian Universalist congregation established in 1796.*

Acknowledgments

I have been privileged to learn from and collaborate with a remarkable number of generous people over the past twelve years. The result is *Exorcising Preaching*.

My colleagues at Chalice Press have been a delight to work with. Brad Lyons, Gail Stobaugh, Steve Knight, and KJ Reynolds are professionals par excellence; in particular, I am honored to learn from the expertise of Bill Watkins whose editorial feedback strengthened the manuscript and bettered my character.

I am also grateful for the support of Dudley Rose at Harvard Divinity School for sponsoring my preaching seminar on this subject, and to the members of HUUMS, Harvard Unitarian Universalist Ministry for Students, for their inspiring worship services.

I am indebted to the liberating pedagogy and inspirational theology of the preaching and worship faculty at Union Theological Seminary—Janet Walton, Barbara Lundblad, and Troy Messenger. Attending Union was a freeing and challenging experience. I will never forget James Cone passionately saying, "You've got to find your voice." *Exorcising Preaching* is one step in that lifelong pursuit.

The self-educed exorcisms in this preaching book are a direct result of experimental worship services that I led at the Fourth Universalist Society in the City of New York; Community Unitarian Church at White Plains, New York; the Unitarian Church of Staten Island, New York; and the First Unitarian Church of Philadelphia. I am deeply honored to have had the chance to craft contemporary services in collaboration with the worship associates in those congregations; as they can attest, not all of my experiments worked. I am thankful for their kindness and support, whether my risk-taking bore rewards or blemishes.

I am particularly grateful for the research assistance and collegial advice of Lee Paczulla and Ranwa Hammamy, whose wisdom will aid many for decades to come. I am deeply honored to be a recipient of the collegial support of Ed Greenlee, Addae Ama Kraba, and Zemoria Brandon who encouraged me to articulate my worship theories and experiment with the craft of preaching. I never could have maintained this discipline without my executive coach,

Beverley Rhinesmith-Pape. Week after week for the last six years, she has held me accountable for my goals and compassionately contributed to the development of my self-worth.

This book would never have been possible had it not been for the outstanding copyediting support of my colleagues at Wordy. com, in particular the incomparable Heather Rothman. CEO and founder of Wordy.com, Anders Schepelern, generously gave me a financial discount on editorial services due to my three learning disabilities—dyslexia, a processing delay, and a reading memory deficiency. As an author who now has access to twenty-four-hour copyediting support, I feel that the stigma of being "disabled" is significantly less potent.

My colleagues were another constant source of support. They held me in care and held me accountable for creating systems of ministerial excellence. I thank my mentors: Mark Bellitini for his poetic wisdom; Meg Riley for her prophetic ministry; and Ned Wight for his humor and kindness. Month after month, I had the privilege of meeting with incredibly skillful ministers to whom I will forever be grateful: Ken Beldon, Kathy Ellis, Peter Friedrichs, Kent Matthies, Manish Mishra-Marzetti, and Libby Smith. They taught me that ministry is done not in isolation but in a universal network of mutuality. May all preachers, in all times, have access to kind and generous colleagues.

List of Tables

A Call to Worship

"What happened to her voice?" my colleague asked me while we walked out of our preaching class. I said, "The same thing that happens to nearly all of us when we read sacred text aloud: we become possessed by the ghosts of dead community-theater actors."

It is bizarre but true. Preachers can be possessed. We approach the pulpit, open the text, and then suddenly our speech becomes exaggerated and breathy. The people in the pew cannot help but tilt their heads and say to themselves, "The preacher is really feeling it today." In that moment, a veil separates the preacher and the worshipers. It is not only off-putting and annoying, but this masked delivery also becomes a barrier that prevents worshipers from making meaning. The people come to community to reflect upon their lives, to mourn, to celebrate, but not to be held captive by the pretenses of "the ordained."

I have seen many videos of myself preaching in which I was possessed with that kind of artificial affect. As a gay, white, thirty-something man, it is incredibly awkward to watch me try to sound like James Earl Jones, or worse, Maya Angelou. Enough. It does not work, for anyone. The truth is that unnatural speech is off-putting, pretentious, and condescending.

I do not remember the exact moment, or whether it was a series of moments, but ultimately I decided to exorcise the ghosts of dead community-theater actors from my speech. I was determined to be real when I approached the pulpit. I got out of my own way and simply read the text. I began to decontaminate my sermons of that preachy voice—not always, but most of the time. I had to extricate myself from this bad habit because I knew that effective preaching required my sincere speech and my authentic presence.

This is the first of several examples of how I learned to conduct exorcisms on myself—the subject of this book. Whether preparing or performing a sermon, I have found myself possessed by notions that caused others and me harm. The most common is the mistaken idea that people actually listen to sermons. Most clergy know this cannot be true. That is why I titled the first chapter "No One Is Listening to You." They are not. Worshipers come to listen for that which is *within* and *beyond* them. This is why worshipers often thank preachers for sharing a message the preachers, literally, did not say aloud. But that message is what the worshipers heard. It is a little spooky, but intriguing.

I am interested in preaching that is both timely and timeless. I am attracted to preachers who treat each sermon as if it were their last, and that is the subject of the second chapter, titled "Preach or Die." There is no time for pretense. There is no time for forced joy or frantic desperation. Urgency without joy can be frenetic. Joy without urgency can be sentimental. I am determined to exorcise frothy emotionality and irrelevant theology because I believe that worship is not an errand; it is a privilege. Preaching is a dynamic discipline designed to enhance the faith and develop the morals and intellect of the people and the preacher.

A communal model of preaching has the potential to inspire members of the community to train one another to use their passion and their intellect, their faith and their reason—to collaborate as a single, integrated, and dynamic entity. In the third chapter, I illustrate how members of my community have effectively democratized the pulpit. By actually polling one another about the moral issues of our time, they joined me in brushing off the liturgical dust. Nearly instantly, worshipers exorcised their previous role as spectators and became engaged stakeholders.

In order to achieve these goals I had to constantly ask for help. I needed to banish the idea that my sermons would somehow write themselves on the Saturday night before I was scheduled to preach. The community of stakeholders became my accountability system, the subject of the fourth chapter. They helped me preempt my tendency to procrastinate. Worship associates and colleagues helped me research, rehearse, and revise my sermons, leaving me time to sleep deeply on (most) Saturday nights. This is also what it means to exorcise preaching: to expel harmful habits, like sleep deprivation, which can keep clergy from having a healthy life/work balance.

In addition to these self-care practices, the craft of preaching also requires intellectual honesty, the interlocking theme to the fifth and sixth chapters: "Exile Theological and Pastoral Clichés" and "Purge Theological Violence." Clergy have long since recognized that God-talk born from banal platitudes diminishes the power of theology. I strive to emancipate myself from such practices, beginning by taking the vow to only speak for myself. I will not speak for God, for scriptures, or on behalf of any religious community. Using "I" statements allows me to lay the foundation to transform theological clichés into hard-won lessons that lay claim to no celestial rewards. I do not claim to know if "everything happens for a reason" or if a tragedy is really "a blessing in disguise." Exiling these kinds of stock phrases is one step in my attempt to develop a principled, trustworthy ministerial identity.

Another step is to purge all forms of theological violence from my thoughts, words, and deeds. I do so by making the promise to train myself in how to responsibly consume and analyze religious passages that are inherently violent. I consider these passages to be *texts of terror*—verses that have been misused by some religious leaders to justify oppression and to make theological threats. Preachers who believed that they had the power to speak for God, for the Bible, and for a "one, true religion," have been possessed by theological vanity and have been propagators of theological despair.

Aware of the suffering caused by these harmful practices, I am determined to be a preacher who seeks to dethrone myself from the center of the world and to purge from my character all notions of religion-based bigotry. As the "Charter for Compassion" proposes, I vow to deem "any interpretation of scripture that breeds violence, hatred or disdain [to be] illegitimate" (full text can be found at www.CharterForCompassion.org). I believe that if religious leaders were to exorcise violence from our communities, then religions of many colors could help return the Golden Rule to the center of religious, moral, and political life. Treating others as I want to be treated is one way I can responsibly interpret the religious violence in scriptures—violence that I vow to never propagate.

To effectively communicate this vision, I cannot use the same stale preaching form week after week. Not all content can be delivered in the same way, a point that I illustrate with a number of examples in the seventh, and final, chapter. The process of replacing the one-note sermon with a symphony of forms results in a diversity of preaching styles that helps keep the worship services fresh. And that is the task before the contemporary preacher: to use healing spiritual disciplines to reawaken the craft for clergy and congregants. For instance, study is a common spiritual practice, which requires me to contemplate the nature of my source texts and the impact my interpretations may have on others. In this way, the art of developing a sermon is a process-based discipline coupled with other types of spiritual practices that may determine the product. How the content is shared is just as important as what I choose to share. Some of my sermons are best prayed, others sung, while some sermons take on the form of a story and still others unravel the complexities of moral dilemmas. Each sermon form must be intimately woven with the content, so that I do not end up saying different things but in the same old way. By using spiritual practices to marry both content *and* form, I have been told that each of my sermons are distinct and unique. This has helped me keep worship services alive from one week to the next.

Exorcising Preaching promises to save preachers from harmful habits by learning the methods they can use to liberate themselves and their communities. In this narrative, I illustrate how I have attempted to expel unhealthy practices with gritty exorcisms. I do so in three ways: by reflecting on my relationship to the craft of preaching, by embedding excerpts of my sermons in some of the chapters to reinforce those lessons learned, and by including in the Appendices full sermons to demonstrate how these various techniques result in a diversity of sermons. My hope is that this book will ultimately inspire readers—not to adopt my exorcisms, but rather to document their own.

I plan to make this the first of a book series with a companion website, www.ExorcisingPreaching.com. There, preachers can submit their own exorcisms. I will edit some of them into a second book designed to feature spirited lessons about preaching in multicultural and multigenerational communities. My hope is that this series can be used as textbooks in seminaries, guidebooks for clergy, and workbooks for religious communities.

In this first volume, it is important for me to convey an essential ground rule: one person cannot exorcise another person. Exorcisms need to be self-induced. The illustrations in this book come from years of my own attempts at banishing the harmful patterns that diminished my craft and my potential. My problems and my solutions are my own. I do not assume that they will ring true for others, because I know my colleagues are wrestling with their own demons. The primary gift of this book is not necessarily the content, but rather the method.

I will know if *Exorcising Preaching* is successful, not when my colleagues are implementing my exorcisms, but when they are creating their own. It is the technique of exorcising thyself that promises to liberate the preacher. The warnings I share in this text are archives of my evolving guidelines; they are not to be used as a universal guidebook for all. This is why I use this introduction to invite preachers to experiment with their own exorcisms and to share what they have learned. My ultimate purpose is for the

Exorcising Preaching series to serve as a vocational catalyst for preachers in a diversity of religious communities to engage in rigorous self-analysis and theological reflection about the art of preaching.

Just as I have exorcised the idea that worshipers listen to me when I preach, I expect a similar outcome with this book. I invite student and seasoned preachers to read, not with the intent to study my words, but to listen to that which is *within* and *beyond* them. In those moments, preachers will be called to excavate the wisdom that had been held captive by harmful habits. May these graphic exorcisms, the ones I present here and the ones you are about to create, have the power to liberate the preacher, the pulpit, and the people.

1

No One Is Listening to You

❖ ❖ ❖ "Have I shared with you my preaching philosophy?" I asked the gathered congregation. I said, "It's simple: Nate, no one is listening to you." Folks chuckled. I replied, "I mean it. The people come not to listen to the preacher. They come to listen for that which is within and beyond them." The congregation stilled as I said, "Let us begin." ❖

When I began my preaching career, I routinely felt myself confused that congregants were not really hearing what I had to say. Churchgoers would often thank me for a sermon I did not preach—an experience, I have come to learn, that happens to preachers more often than not.

"Your sermon about forgiveness brought me to tears," a woman said while hugging me. Clara, we will call her, was a short, stocky woman in her late seventies.

I patted her back while thinking, "That was not about forgiveness. It was about the Sanitary Commission." I had told the story of how Unitarians, such as Thomas Starr King, Henry Whitney Bellows, Samuel Howe, Louisa May Alcott, and Peter Cooper, raised money and organized volunteers to care for the ill and injured soldiers during the Civil War. I was certain that my sermon was not about forgiveness.

A few months later, while in a lobby of a nursing home, I watched Clara's hands slightly tremor, as they always did, while pouring water into a paper Dixie cup. She offered the hospice nurse the water while saying, "Thank you for taking such good care of my husband." Later, when Clara and I were sitting in silence, she said out of nowhere, "I just can't stop thinking about how those Unitarians tended to the wounded soldiers from both the North and the South." Curious, I asked her to elaborate. Then it all began to make sense. For years, members of her husband's family had been caught in the death grip of conflict. She felt triangulated and pressured to choose sides. As her husband became increasingly ill, she came to realize that she could play another role in the family system: to tend to the wounds carried by both factions. As one who married into the family, Clara realized she needed not be enlisted in either camp. She learned to be a caregiver to both. That is why I call her Clara, after Clara Barton, a Unitarian who founded the American Red Cross. This gentle woman taught me that the sermon I intended to be on the Sanitary Commission was, indeed for her, about forgiveness. I learned that those who received my sermons often experienced a different intent than what I sought in writing them.

I will never forget when a church elder beckoned me over to his pew, the same corner of the church he had been sitting in nearly every Sunday for thirty-some years. He said, "Thank you for that invigorating sermon. I am going right home to call my son and tell him he's a spoiled little brat."

I half laughed and half gasped because my sermon was titled "Deep Listening and Loving Speech." I felt devastated. I said, "Ron, the sermon was titled—"

He interrupted. "I know what the sermon was about. But tough love can go a long way."

I could not believe it. A sermon designed to inspire kindness led a cranky elder to leave church armed to confront his adult son. I felt like a failure. I felt even worse when, a year later, his son came both late and drunk to Ron's scantily attended memorial service.

All I wanted were my words to help someone. I wanted to have some impact somewhere, but often the receipts on the communication came back with items that I had not intended to gift to others. I still want my words to help people, but I have different expectations now. I have come to accept the fact that *how* my sermons are received are not entirely under my control, as it should be. Facing this reality transformed my relationship to preaching and freed me of the cage that comes with unrealistic expectations. This allowed me to ask a new question: How do I communicate with people, knowing that what I say is not what is always heard? This inquiry began my renewed relationship with the craft of preaching and allowed me to have a more realistic pastoral relationship with parishioners. It also inspired me to experiment with the various ways to communicate from the pulpit.

In my early years, I started the writing process by whittling down a series of complex ideas into three memorable points—a common preaching form. I summarized them at the beginning, expanded upon them in the middle, and recapped them at the end. That is how sermons were supposed to be written, I thought. I held all kinds of unexamined notions. It was as if I were a political candidate who wanted my constituents to know my campaign's three priorities. Or it was as if I were a professor who was planning to issue a pop quiz at the end of the month, testing my students' retention of my previous lectures. I had to get honest with myself. I am not a politician. I am not a lecturer. I am a minister, a preacher. But no matter how hard I tried to be heard, I could not predetermine what messages my congregants received. I had no other choice but to let go of the outcome. At first, I was perplexed by this reality. Then the act of letting go liberated my process and my performance. I kept saying to myself while writing sermons, "Nate, no one is listening to you. They're just not."

This liberation resulted in a number of outcomes. Mostly, I felt less pressure. I experienced a kind of lightness—a shift in the dense mood that, unbeknownst to me, had been clouding my ministry. This unchartered process of writing with the intent *not to be heard* ultimately freed me. Letting go did not mean to disassociate or detach; it was quite the opposite. Letting go meant leaning in. I began actively listening to congregants while I was speaking. Literally, while preaching, I found myself leaning into the congregation. I no longer needed a receipt on whether or not they heard me. Rather, I sought to hear them. I leaned into the worshipers with the intent to imagine the different ways this and that story met with their realities.

This resulted in a different quality to our nonverbal exchanges during worship. I experienced deeper intimacy with the community by really looking into its eyes, as if they were stained-glass images of the members' lives. Although the congregants were facing me, I had the privilege of watching them. I always had the best seat in the house.

Preaching became a multilayered experience. I began to read more than the sermon. I was literally sharing my words, but I was also reading their lives: the woman in the back who had just filed for divorce, the man in green who had been laid off, the couple from

Florida who had welcomed another grandchild, the visitors who had found the courage to try something new, and the law student who had found time to make it to church.

I came to understand that the people arrived not to hear me preach but to experience that which lay *within* and *beyond* them. I am not sure if I fully know what I mean when I say that. *Within* is a poetic way to describe the rich internal life of the worshiper. Some Unitarian Universalists are theists with vibrant prayer lives who have a personal and intimate relationship with their experience of the Divine. Some use the word God, others speak directly to Brother Jesus, and others talk with their deceased loved ones. Theological diversity is the norm (Appendix A). Others in the congregation have not experienced a supernatural presence, but have vast imaginations leading them to experience mystery, wonder, and awe. Their internal lives are rich with curiosity and creativity and sometimes occupied by fears of unknown calamities—fears not driven by supernaturalism but by political unrest and environmental degradation. When the gathered community is that theologically diverse, worship becomes an opportunity to learn from one another's differences rather than to reinforce the preacher's ideas and beliefs. Meditation and prayer, for instance, is a time when different people respectively engage in different spiritual practices. Some actually pray. Some sit in silence. My role is not to coerce any of them into any particular practice but to simply give them the space to be authentic. In this time, many struggle with making lists in their heads or replaying the lead roles in the dramas of their lives. As a worship leader, I hope to simply craft a time and place in which anyone who gathers with us can experience the meaningful *within* moments that seem to transcend any sense of time.

One of the great privileges of ministry has been when worshipers grant me access to their private lives. In both formal and informal pastoral exchanges, congregants have given me glimpses into how they pray, or why they do not. They have recounted times when they first believed, times when their beliefs have changed, and times when harsh realities and disenchantment transformed faith into fiction. They have taught me that grief can fuel both faith and disbelief. They have welcomed me into their sanctuary, which led me to bow in reverence for their direct experience of all that which is *within* them.

Worshipers have also taught me they come to church to get out of their heads. When feeling bad, they want to be inspired to do good. They want to be in the world, engaged and poised to make some difference for someone, somewhere. People crave an aesthetic experience that moves them *beyond* their limited existence and calls them to action. They long to be awakened into a new way of being in the world, based on being highly informed citizens of the world. They long for transformation and connection and for some affirmation that they are not isolated beings in a sea of social anonymity. They want to feel that unexplainable connection to one another and to all that is holy.

In these ways I have come to realize that it is true: "Nate, no one is listening to you." Truly. Nor should they be. The people come to listen to that which is *within* and *beyond* them. My role as preacher is not to be heard; it is to be a witness to that which is *within* and *beyond* all those who gather. It is a great privilege to be invited into people's vast internal sanctuaries. Consequently, when I enter the physical sanctuary of our church with my fellow sojourners, I come simply to let them know in nonverbal ways that they are the ones being heard, they are the ones who are seen—they belong, and they matter to me and to the community. I may literally be the one speaking, but their lives have my full attention.

Then there were the days when people actually listened to me. Imagine!

I dedicate the remaining part of this chapter to sharing with you an extended excerpt from a sermon that I delivered—one that some people actually heard.

I will never forget that Easter Sunday after Pope Benedict resigned and Pope Francis was installed in 2013. I titled my sermon "The Future of the Catholic Church." In the weeks leading up to the service, I invited Facebookers to share their predictions. Then someone asked, "Reverend Nate, why are you preaching about the Catholic Church?" The answer became the opening line of my sermon.

"Where do ex-Catholics in Philadelphia go for Easter? The First Unitarian Church, of course," I said. "So if this is the first and only time you'll be here all year, welcome. This is the day for you."

I chose this topic because I knew I would be welcoming many people who were raised Catholic or were once practicing Catholics. I designed the first part of the sermon to set a framework and to explain the demographic context for my challenge. I began this way:

To engage this topic with some intellectual honesty, let's set one ground rule. There is no such thing as *the* Catholic Church. Rather, there are a plethora of Catholicisms, plural. There are geographically defined Catholicisms, such as the Roman Catholic Church, which is strikingly different from the Armenian Catholic Church. There are theologically distinct Catholicisms, such as Opus Dei as compared with the Franciscans. And there are politically distinct Catholicisms, such as the Ethiopian Catholic Church in contrast with the American "Nuns on the Bus."

As you can see, I already broke the ground rule. The correct title of my sermon should not read "The Future of *the* Catholic Church." It should read "The Future of Catholicisms."

What do we know about Catholicisms? Half of the global Christian population identifies with some branch of it—that equates to 1.1 billion adherents worldwide. In the United States, Catholics represent 24 percent of the population; they hold 30 percent of the seats in Congress and six of the nine seats on the U.S. Supreme Court. The other seats on the high court are held by Jews, with no Protestant represented. This makes the upcoming gay marriage cases that much more interesting, given the strong role that various Catholic groups have played in legally defining marriage between one man and one woman.

According to the Pew Research Center, the American Catholic Church "has lost more members over the past few decades than any other major religion." The top reason for this mass exodus is the clergy sex-abuse scandals. Also, nearly six in ten of those who stopped identifying with any form of Catholicism left because of their "dissatisfaction with Catholic teachings on abortion and homosexuality; about half cite concerns about Catholic teachings on birth control." There is also the longstanding conflict regarding the role of women in leadership positions.

What do all these topics have in common? Sex. The modern sex inquisitions against women and gays are shockingly contradictory to the secretive protections granted to sex offenders in the priesthood. The chronic harm done to generations and generations of children, women, and homosexuals leaves current members of Catholic churches no other choice than to democratize their traditions. The basis for this reform is simple: sexual ethics. Undertaking this reform may be salvation for many Catholic communities.

I proceeded to substantiate these claims by discussing celibacy, conjugal marriage, roles of women, and sexual abuse. This gave me the contextual justification for the remedy of democratic reform.

Specific to the subject of this *exorcise* on *no one is listening to you*, I proceeded to preach a multilayered message: the most outer layer many people actually heard, which surprised me, but there was a private audience, too. I said:

The most effective way to sanctify the many branches of Catholicism is to democratize the churches. Yes, democratize the churches. Hold on to your pews because this here is your Easter message of resurrection.

For all of you ex-Catholics who came here today seeking healing from your religious past, know that we are honored to be in your presence. But let me be honest: our society does not need you to become one of us. We need you to face your religious past—go home. I mean it. Go home. Occupy the pews. Organize. Strategize and democratize the Catholic churches.

For far too long, Catholic institutions have been held in the death grip of feudalism—a hierarchal system of governance that has led to their demise. The remedy is to dilute concentrated power; the remedy is to decentralize systems that were designed for totalitarian control; the remedy is to de-gender the patriarchal priesthood and to demand that every church be a true sanctuary for the most vulnerable among us—children.

In doing so, you will be able to work together with the many skillful priests and nuns who have dedicated their lives to co-create systems of accountability and integrity based on principles of transparency and human decency.

Go to those priests and nuns who are doing the good work of reform. Bring your concerns, build relationships with your bishops who want to restore the churches' role in the community, and regularly communicate your experiences to your new Pope. Articulate not only what you are against but also what you find practical. Then find timely ways to manifest what you are for. By democratizing your churches, you will exorcize the sins of invidious discrimination, exclusion, and oppression. This is made possible when you marry the sacred practice of restoration with the sacrament of redemption. Only then will you no longer see yourself as a victim of a broken past. You will look into the mirror and see that *you,* you are the remedy to create a vision of health and wholeness. By democratizing the churches, you will soon become co-creators of your creeds. You will join in creating not only institutional reform but also theological reform.

All you have to do is share the good news that 93 percent of American Catholics believe that people of other religions can go to heaven—universal salvation. Either that means that only 7 percent of American Catholics are in right relationship with the catechism, or maybe it means that Catholics believe that God not only speaks through scripture and priests but through the people, too. Tell the religious leaders of the churches that a super majority of parents do not look at their newborn children and conclude that there is original sin. Petition for the removal of the doctrine of original sin and co-create a Universalist theology of original blessing. Explain that many Catholics believe that God is too good to damn the child, just as God is too good to exclude your lesbian sister from communion, your Muslim fiancé from the sacrament of marriage, and your sister, an unmarried pregnant teacher, from employment.

By democratizing the Catholic churches, you will help create incremental moments of institutional reform based on a new era of theological enlightenment. From out of the Dark Ages and into the twilight of hope, you will join with effective co-creators in sparking a fundamental shift in the church's relationship with civil society.

- No longer will churches say that their religious freedom is infringed when the dogma itself is designed to infringe the rights of women.
- No longer will private religious schools say that their right to practice their faith means it is ethical to terminate homosexuals and unmarried pregnant women from employment.
- No longer will churches say their religious liberties are denied when their dogma justifies them to deny civil liberties to gays and lesbians and transgender people.
- No longer will the church hold the view that their religious laws are above civil laws, secretly shuffling sexual predators from one parish to the next.
- No longer will they see their leaders as infallible or immune from laws designed to protect children and vulnerable adults.
- No longer will the church mischaracterize freedom as a zero-sum game.

True freedom is not jealous. True freedom is not envious. True freedom is not spiteful. True freedom does not desire to restrict the freedoms of others. True freedom knows not a selfish thought, knows not how to threaten. To know true freedom is to know that your win is my glory and that your suffering is inextricably tied to my own. For, the sum of all that is holy shines far beyond our picket signs and our court dockets.

So, if you came wanting a clear and definitive answer to the question about the future of Catholicisms, know that the answer is found in one word: *you*. You are the future. If from these churches you or your ancestors once came, then it's time to go home. Go home and democratize your communities.

And for those who have no immediate tie to any form of Catholicism, know that you, too, are the future of Catholic churches. If one out of every seven people in the world identifies as Catholic, then we are all relative stakeholders. Let's give our neighbors a hand.

So on this Easter, on this day of rebirth and renewal, may we follow the example of Pope Francis and kick off the fancy red slippers and renounce the fancy quarters. There's no time for pretense. It's time to live simply, to feed the poor, and to wash the feet of the prisoners.

May we all play one part in the vision cast by St. Francis of Assisi 800 years ago: "We have been called to heal wounds, to unite what has fallen apart, and to bring home those who have lost their way."

I was surprised by how many people approached me after the service and demonstrated that they had actually listened. Many people thanked me for the challenging message. One visitor said, "I know a priest who is doing what you suggest. I always thought he was a loner, but if more of us supported him, maybe there would be some change." She then said, "In the meantime, I will send a check to support *this* church."

Another visitor said intensely, "Shouldn't some things just die?" and another said, "How dare you tell me to return to *that* place. You really have no idea, do you?" I clearly offended her and I felt ashamed.

The most piercing comment came from a longtime member of the church. She looked me in the eye, shook her head, and said, "You want me to go home? You want me to go home?" She was a former Catholic nun who had left her order and found refuge in the Unitarian Universalist community some forty years earlier. She was angry and upset that I would make such a cruel suggestion. I could see why it was so off-putting and I apologized.

My message was inspiring to some and insulting to others—a tough reality to accept. Some welcomed the challenge, and others simply wanted to be welcomed. In all cases, they heard what I had to say but interpreted it through the lens of their own lives. They were listening to that which was *within* them, and, in some contexts, that which was *beyond* them was utterly terrifying.

I empathized with every comment across the spectrum. I respected those who were doing the good work of democratic reform, and I had compassion for those who were insulted by the challenge. I related to them all because I had witnessed a dear colleague of mine go through extreme situations in his church. So, when he told me he was coming that that Easter service, I knew he would be truly listening to me.

While in seminary, I was mentored by an adjunct professor who began his ministry ten years earlier. He taught a couple of classes while working at an Episcopalian church in Long Island. We will call him Taylor. Taylor's church was known as an "after-pastor congregation," a term designated to communities whose previous clergy had engaged in serious misconduct, sexual or otherwise. In such systems, long-term members have not had the chance (or reason) to learn to trust clergy. In his church, two previous male priests had been fired for having sexual relationships with married women in the church, and Taylor's most immediate predecessor was fired for abuse of alcohol—literally, for preaching drunk. In this program-sized suburban congregation, members' aggression against ministers became the norm. It became a survival mechanism for the community to withstand three decades of abuse.

When Taylor began his ministry, he was the target of a number of physical and sexual aggressions. In his first year, a deacon in the church posted a warning sign for a seminarian that said, "If you don't return these Bibles, I will cut you and set you on fire ." When Taylor asked this deacon, "Did you write this?" the person responded, "Don't think priests are exempt from being cut." When Taylor brought this to the board's attention in the form of a written memo, the trustees made no verbal or written acknowledgment of this event. He brought it up in another Board meeting and, again, received no response. Taylor ultimately asked the aggressor to leave the church, to which two trustees responded by splitting their pledge in half and publicly giving it as a cash gift to the person leaving. Taylor felt even more troubled. His employers were not committed to ensuring a safe work environment, and two supervisors were actively rewarding those who made it a hostile workplace. He used this incident as a case study in a class he taught us in seminary about after-pastor congregations, demonstrating how long-term members can develop a habit of being "clergy killers."

Taylor also experienced chronic sexual aggressions. One former trustee said in a meeting, "I'm having a hard time concentrating on your sermons."

He asked, "Oh yeah? Why is that?"

She said, "I keep undressing you with my eyes."

Taylor told me that he nearly fainted. Instead, he said, "It's not uncommon for people to sexualize those in positions of authority. But you know the secret to public speaking, don't you?...picture everyone naked." They laughed. I thought he managed the situation quite well. But Taylor was troubled by the fact that none of the six leaders who witnessed this aggression ever checked in with him or confronted the person who had made the comment. This is a symptom, Taylor knew, of an after-pastor congregation.

Over the years, Taylor felt more and more unsafe in his workplace. He was constantly thinking of leaving congregational ministry. He later moved to another church outside of Trenton, New Jersey. There he caught an employee, a relative of a trustee, embezzling thousands of dollars. When Taylor reported this to the police, some church leaders chastised him for not keeping it buried in the name of protecting the church's image.

I met up with Taylor a few months after this difficulty, when he was on sabbatical. Over lunch he told me that he was considering resigning because he was tired of working for people who were complacent to abuse. He felt like the system was stacked against him. He was even considering renouncing his ordination altogether. He wanted to stay, he told me, but did not know if he had the stamina to go back for another round.

We took a long walk along the Schuylkill River when he told me that he was planning to come to my Easter service. I asked him, "What kind of message would you like to hear?" He paused and said, "I'm looking for a sign to know whether to stay or leave congregational ministry."

I learned long ago that preachers not only preach to the congregation as a whole but also to the individuals who have come for pastoral care sessions the weeks preceding. In this context, Taylor was aware of his internal impulse to flee. He was looking for a compelling reason to stay in congregational ministry, but was doubtful about its probable success. I, therefore, designed my sermon with two audiences in mind: the ex-Catholics and Taylor. Or maybe it was one audience: all those lovers of leaving. Regardless of how many audiences, there was only one message: "Face your religious past—go home. I mean it. Go home. Occupy the pews. Organize. Strategize and democratize your church."

I wanted Taylor to know that he did not have to give up his power to bullies. I wanted Taylor to know that Catholic churches were experiencing far greater violations and that the issues he faced were much more manageable. He had the authority and the respect to lead in a time of vulnerability. After all, my message was simply a reflection of what he taught so many of us in seminary. Taylor's teachings and his story inspired me to proclaim, "Marry the sacred practice of restoration with the sacrament of redemption. You are not a victim of a broken past. You are but one part of the remedy to a vision of health and wholeness."

What was his response to the Easter sermon? He bear hugged me and said, "Students are always the best teachers." A year later, he wrote me a letter explaining why he decided to leave congregational ministry and pursue denominational leadership. He said, "Here's to being a guardian of health and wholeness." He signed it with his new title, "Bishop."

I came to believe that preaching and worship can be powerful tools to help restore communities to a state of balance. I decided to use the Easter message to proclaim that challenge for my unique audience of ex-Catholics. Inline with exorcising the desire to be heard I hoped the Easter sermon would allow Taylor to hear himself and ultimately help him transform his feelings of being a victim into being a change agent. This goal was not without its consequences—who would have guessed that this would be the day that people would hear the sermon.

Some people were offended by this message and rightfully insulted that I would suggest they return to an abusive home. I learned that bold generalizations could lack truth in some contexts. Knowing the lives of some of those people, I did my best to apologize. I could see how, in their internal sanctuary, my message was offensive. In Taylor's, it was empowering. This complexity reveals one layer of power behind preaching: to engage an aesthetic expression that can create for the listeners a diversity of experiences of that which is *within* and *beyond* them. That process may strike a painful nerve for some and may tap a deep well of wisdom for those whose parched sense of safety have been lost to an oasis of despair.

Preachers are not exempt from this intimate complexity. Messages can spring from wells deep within us—designed for us, too. I had also been in a vulnerable time that Easter season, questioning my own call to ministry. It is a question that many lovers of leaving ask themselves. Looking back, I wonder if Taylor and the Easter ex-Catholics were the audiences of my conscious mind, whereas I was the audience of my subconscious. I suppose that I was the one who needed to be reminded how to stand by this faith. In this way, there is another layer of truth to the exorcism: "Nate, no one is listening to you—even yourself." Funny how I tried but failed to hear the words that came from my own mouth.

I do not expect or recommend that preachers in other traditions, even other Unitarian Universalist ministers, adopt my preaching philosophy that *no one is listening to you*. I urge them to develop their own philosophy and then share it publicly. Some of my colleagues who come from Bible-based traditions believe that, when they are speaking, the Holy Spirit is preaching. They see themselves as channels through which God is preaching a saving message. They, too, may not believe that they are to be heard, but rather that God is to be understood. Different theologies and different philosophies of preaching create different results and effects. I do not recommend that preachers, even in my own tradition, adopt my own views. The purpose of this opening chapter is to illustrate a method by which we, as preachers, can name that which we want to purge from the craft and what helpful habits we want to cultivate.

For me, I chose to improve the craft—at least my view and practice of it—by exorcising two ideas: first, the myth that people were listening to me preach, and, second, that clergy are not their own audience. Once I had purged these notions from the craft of preaching, I felt liberated. I started to take the first steps into a new vocational process. Once I had come to accept that delivering sermons was a distinct form of public speaking, I began the process of exorcising the craft. I began to shed the unexamined need to be heard and challenged myself to hear myself. Other preachers may not reach this same conclusion. Their challenges are different from my own, just as their lessons will be.

That is why this first volume of *Exorcising Preaching* is designed to archive my experiences, whereas future volumes will disseminate lessons shared by colleagues from a wide range of religious traditions. *Exorcising Preaching* is not simply a book; it is a ministerial process. Each of us in our own way has learned to exorcise—to purge, to cleanse, to cast out, to purify—the notions that either keep us from reaching our potential or ideas that keep us from harming ourselves and others. The challenge before us is to archive those lessons and to collectively reform the entire discipline.

2

Preach or Die

❖ ❖ ❖ The craft of preaching requires both urgency and joy.
Urgency without joy can be frenetic. Joy without urgency
can be sentimental. Preach as if it is your last sermon. Drop
the idea that the sermon is an errand. Preaching is a dynamic
discipline designed to enhance the moral, intellectual, and
faith development of the people and the preacher. ❖

In May 1838, Pennsylvania Hall, an abolitionist meeting place
in Philadelphia, was burned to the ground. In response, William
Henry Furness (1802–1896), the first minister of the historic First
Unitarian Church, delivered what was likely his first public sermon
that revealed his objection to slavery. Admittedly, he avoided the
subject for the first thirteen years of his tenure, calling himself "an
eleventh-hour man." One of the pressures he faced was that some
of the members were slave owners, most notably Pierce Butler, the
heir to the estate of U.S. Senator Pierce Butler of South Carolina,
one of the nation's largest cotton-plantation proprietors.

Incrementally, Furness ('fərnəs or *furnace*) made the subject of
slavery an incidental theme in his early sermons, which ignited
members to organize a public rebellion against him in 1841. Even
members sympathetic to his cause petitioned for his cessation of his
antislavery comments. Others called for his immediate resignation.
The following year, trustees declared that their bylaws prevented
them from controlling or interfering with the minister's official
duties. Furness publicly responded by saying, "When I feel myself
bound, as I do, to utter ungracious truth, to speak what it offends

and pains you to hear, it is one of the very hardest duties that I have ever undertaken to perform." Ultimately, the congregation split into two as a critical mass of members withdrew their financial support and resigned from the church.

The threats were so severe that two of Furness's friends came to church on Sundays with "loaded pistols in their pockets to defend him to the uttermost," wrote Furness's son, Horace. The stakes were so high that when Furness spoke against the 1850 Fugitive Slave Law, President James Buchannan's administration considered indicting Furness for treason.

As a contemporary minister installed to preach from Furness's historic pulpit, I could not help but regularly ask myself, "What sermon might I preach this week that would require my protectors to carry firearms? What moral subject would require such urgency that I would be faced with the challenge to preach or die?"

"Live free or die," revolutionaries have cried. "Vote or die," organizers have chanted. These hyperboles express urgency for collective action, a call to what Martin Luther King Jr. often described as "the fierce urgency of now." Precisely one year before his assassination, King proclaimed the following words in protest of the American Vietnam War:

> We are now faced with the fact that tomorrow is today. We are confronted with the fierce urgency of now. In this unfolding conundrum of life and history there is such a thing as being too late. Procrastination is still the thief of time. Life often leaves us standing bare, naked and dejected with a lost opportunity. The "tide in the affairs of men" does not remain at the flood; it ebbs. We may cry out desperately for time to pause in her passage, but time is deaf to every plea and rushes on. Over the bleached bones and jumbled residue of numerous civilizations are written the pathetic words: "Too late." There is an invisible book of life that faithfully records our vigilance or our neglect. "The moving finger writes, and having writ moves on..." We still have a choice today; nonviolent coexistence or violent co-annihilation.
>
> We must move past indecision to action. We must find new ways to speak for peace in Vietnam and justice throughout the developing world—a world that borders on our doors. If we do not act we shall surely be dragged down the long dark and

shameful corridors of time reserved for those who possess power
without compassion, might without morality, and strength
without sight.[1]

When Martin Luther King Jr. was a student at Crozer Seminary, outside of Philadelphia, he visited the historic First Unitarian Church. He attended a lecture about Henry David Thoreau's theory of civil disobedience. (Thoreau, Ralph Waldo Emerson, and William Furness were close friends.) The speakers recounted how Mohandas Gandhi, via the writings of Leo Tolstoy, was inspired to couple Thoreau's theory of civil disobedience with *satyagraha* (Sanskrit for "insistence on truth")—the spiritual basis for nonviolence. Allegedly, this lecture is where King first learned of nonviolent civil disobedience. This may explain why, while pursuing his doctorate, King attended a Unitarian church in Boston where he met his wife Coretta. It may also explain why there were more Unitarian clergy in the Selma marches than any other religious tradition.

When reflecting upon the history of our living tradition, I often ask myself, "Who will enter the sanctuary today? What idea could we explore that would inspire someone to make peace and justice not simply a political slogan but a way of life?" At times, these questions gave me a sense of urgency. But over the years, I felt this urgency wane.

In looking down the corridors of time, back at the sermons I have preached, I cannot help but notice how the quality of some was eclipsed by the quantity of what I was expected to produce. Week after week I faced the dilemma that all preachers eventually confront: the privilege and the pressure of needing to create new works regularly.

In the first season of my ministry, I finished each year with a list of unpreached sermon topics. I carried some subjects over from one year to the next. Ultimately, I found myself depleted and uninspired, and every once in a while, I recycled old sermons. (Thankfully, no one was listening to me!) I had no other choice than to confront the drought-stricken winter of writer's block. The honor of preaching had become another box to check on the exhausting list of a week in the life of a congregational minister.

In these times, doubt began to shine through the cracks of people's compliments. "Provocative sermon. You really got me thinking," a member would say. I saw members speak, but I did not listen. I smiled and thanked them as the echoes of their intended meaning were twisted in the tunnels of my mind. I filtered their praise through my fatigue. When people said, "Nice work, Nate," I heard, "Too late."

I felt as if I had become "an eleventh-hour man," failing to address matters of real significance. The sermons were fine, and some were good, but in the end, most simply served their function and filled the space. "But, but, but," became the hidden chant of self-doubt. "Where's the fire in your belly?" I asked myself. Intellectually, I knew that not all of my sermons needed to be driven by a fierce urgency. Some were better motivated by plodding grief or by thawing wonder or by studying an unwavering inner stillness. Yet, I felt as though the craft had become an errand.

I imagine many professionals eventually face this dilemma. How many Broadway performers go into autopilot week after week, how many Olympians let their muscle memory take over, and how many teachers press an internal play button when faced with another semester? Being a professional implies that you not only know how to perform under pressure, but that you have the internal stamina to perform with consistency. I learned to be a reliable preacher, but I worried about being constantly uninspired.

I do not want to imply that every sermon needed to win an award—just ask composers how many of their songs were hits. I am not necessarily talking about the ultimate product of what I delivered but rather the energy that I put into the creative process. My lament was not about preaching less-than-perfect sermons but about having preached with such regularity that I allowed my process to be stultified by the thief of time. My apathy had become calcified. The everyday drudgery led me to feel distanced from my own training. Ultimately, I enrolled in my own miseducation and assigned self-exorcisms, namely, *preach or die.*

I will never forget the preachers at the Poverty Truth Commission. As seminarians, we raised funds through the Poverty Initiative at Union Theological Seminary to hire people to deliver sermons about their direct experience with homelessness and chronic unemployment. Their sermons were so powerful and profound that the gathered congregation wailed with unbridled fervor. Stomping, clapping, cheering—the preachers treated their sermons as if they were their first and last chance to speak truth to power. The event ultimately led them to claim their own power.

It was one of the most profound experiences in my ministerial formation process.

Years later, I found myself replaying this memory while in my ministerial office. Looking out onto Chestnut Street, I saw my homeless neighbors sitting on the church porch. Rather than feel equipped to help them right then and there, or to preach about economic and other injustices, I felt imprisoned by the drudgery of congregational ministry. I was imprisoned by internal preoccupations about curtains, coffee supplies, and policy clauses—these were the agendas that had come to infect my days.

Depleted and uninspired, I felt I no longer had the right to partake in the rite of preaching. Others, I believed, were better poised and more prepared to enliven the people to collective action. My despair was a result of chronic disenchantment, a state of being that my mentors warned me would ebb and flow throughout a preacher's career. We are not all "on" all the time.

I eventually broke the spell by asking, "What if this were my last sermon?" I wrote this question on an index card and taped it to my office wall. I wrote it on my hand. I spoke it aloud. At first, it felt like I was putting more pressure on myself to walk a tightrope while it was being raised higher and higher. I eventually cut out that scene from the film reel in my mind. Focusing, I learned to see that the question did not need to evoke overwhelming feelings but instead a profound sense of freedom. I was free from the weight of having to preach thirty-one more sermons before my next vacation. I was free to focus on the singular task that lay before me. This freedom came with a profound responsibility.

In May 2011, I finally did what James Cone told me to do: I found my voice. And I found it in an unlikely place: a question—"Is liberal religion a saving faith?" With a newfound vigor I preached while the congregation erupted with emotions; they stopped and they howled. I elicited this reaction by claiming that the primary question is not, "What happens when we die?" but "What happens when we kill three times a day?" This was how I revealed the true subject of my sermon—ethical eating. When weighing the risks of preaching such a bold message, I placed less concern on the fear of people walking out or organizing protests. I accepted the challenge to speak on a contemporary topic that would be worthy of preaching from William Furness' pulpit and worthy of experiencing in a sanctuary where Martin Luther King Jr. once learned about nonviolence. I fully accepted the challenge to preach or die and I was dumbfounded by the result: 52 new members joined the church, two of whom led the community the following year to adopt "Ethical Eating" as the congregation's primary social justice theme. The following is an extended excerpt from this breakout sermon. (Listen to the congregation's responses to this sermon by watching the video at www.ExorcisingPreaching.com.)

Is liberal religion a saving faith? If by "saving" you mean that salvation occurs when saying magic words, then nope, we are not a "saving" faith. If by "saving" you mean that we use theology as a spiritual commodity to grant supernatural exemptions in exchange for material tithing, then nope, we're not a "saving" faith. If by "saving," you mean that our theology permits us to exile family members, to persecute our neighbors, to deny civil rights, or to justify violence, then nope, we are not a "saving" faith. Our progressive religion is not concerned with irrelevant questions about insubstantial creeds. Why? Because we do not have time. We do not have time to pontificate about nonsensical inquiries, not because the alleged rapture is near—it is because we cannot tolerate any more acts of exclusion, oppression, violence, and fear.

Are we a people who long to be saved? Hell, yeah! "Save us! Save us," we cry! "Save us from beliefs that suppress! Save us from theologies that don't make sense!" And, "Damn it, save us from religions that coerce!" Save us from the rabbit hole of *woo*—you know, the *woowoo* that leads us into a phantasmagorical wonderland of theological despair. Save us from speculations about the afterlife. Save us from being lured by fantastical thinking about heaven or hell. Save us from whimsical illusions that distract us from the fact that we, as interdependent and limited beings, have the power to create either heaven or hell on earth. The choice is ours. Save us from the hell we create for one another right here, right now. In this way, yes, absolutely, Unitarian Universalism is a saving faith *if* we stop giving new answers to old questions.

How many centuries have religions asked over and over again, "What happens when we die?" We have got to stop this nonsense. None of us knows. The question before us today is not: "What happens when we die?" It is: "What happens when we kill?"

Is it too early in the morning to call for a truly challenging and progressive faith to ask us: "Why do we hire people to kill for us so we can chew on flesh three times a day?" Come on, people—if you like it, clap; if it's offensive, stomp. We gotta wake up those Sunday sleepers with some questions that matter!

What moral and ethical or theological principles do we uphold when we cut into the flesh of another living being? I am serious. I want to know what ethics we uphold when we hire someone to kill animals for our holiday dinner parties.

I started asking these moral questions not because religion taught me to be moral but because my non-religious relatives fed me our pet cow. I thought it was great that we named him McKinley. I was learning about U.S. presidents at the time. I was only eight. Little did I know it was a joke—to feed the children "Big Mac."

How is it that the least religious among us continue to buy into the dominant theological worldview that says that all of this was made for our consumption? How is it that those with secular beliefs fall into the same trap that country club religions are imprisoned by today? It is the prison that says, "It's OK. It doesn't matter what you believe. I'm OK. You're OK. We're all OK. Pass me the A1 sauce—it makes it taste better."

Oh! He shoots, he scores, and the agitated crowd cries, "Don't mess with my A1 sauce!" Listen. I did not come here today to make you feel good. I came here to make you feel alive. So if you're angry, then stomp. If you're humored, then cheer. And for the record, A1 sauce tastes the same on Tofurkey.

Now listen, a truly progressive religion will save us from participating in systems of oppression and violence. A truly redemptive faith will save us from complacency. It will save us from believing that "talking nice" and "smiling pretty" is somehow salvific.

True deliverance will come when we are saved from cultural misappropriation. You know the line: "Well, the Native Americans killed animals." Right. And just as the settlers systemically killed Native Americans, we subsidize three times a day the conquesting systems that profit from suffering.

Oh! He shoots, he scores, while the offended are about to walk out the door as they say, "I wanted to be coddled today by some old-time religion." Well, sorry, kids, not today. It's time to speak truth to power. And you are powerful—you are powerful with your fork three times a day. Will you serve peace on your plate?

Do you think it was easy for William Furness to preach an abolitionist sermon while he had armed guardians at his side? His sermons evoked all kinds of difficult feelings in people.

Let us engage the difficult feelings we are experiencing today as we reflect upon this trend: liberal religion has evolved into a tradition that says, "Don't judge me. I'm OK. We can do and say and believe whatever we want. Let's just talk nice and look pretty." As a result, our so-called liberal religion is not yet liberating us from becoming what we set out against. Rather, it leads us further into despair by permitting—are you ready for this?—moral relativism.

There is a way out of hell, the hell that says killing is OK. "But, but, the chicken was free range," they say. No. This is moral relativism, and it's time we live with moral conviction. If you are going to subsidize violence, at least be intellectually honest. Call it what it is.

If you're going to continue to eat meat—"meat," what an interesting term—if you're going to continue to eat animals based on the traditional argument that we've always done it that way, or the biological argument that humans are designed that way, or the theological argument that Mother Earth provides solely for you...then know that you're doing the same thing that old-time religion does when justifying oppression and violence.

We're told that tradition says, "God made Adam and Eve to procreate. And God gave us dominion over the Earth." That tradition has long told us that women were lesser creatures to men and that the Earth was made for human dominion. The biological argument says that women were made for the sole purpose of procreating, just like Whites were made to be a superior race, right? Just like humans were designed to eat the tender flesh of a young calf, right? It is time we stop plummeting down the rabbit hole that leads us to believe that traditional answers are right and new questions are wrong.

If we really want to build a progressive, prophetic faith, then we cannot solely base our public actions on reactions to oppressive agendas. We must be the ethical agenda-setters of our time. We need to rise up and make a bold and clear stance by saying that religious oppression, religious exclusion, and religious violence are illegitimate—period.

The religious worldview that says, "All of this was made for our consumption," leads to the creation of hell, right here, right now. If we really want to be a part of a liberating, saving community, then we must become a sanctioned, recognized, organized force that will make fundamentalists fall to their knees and repent because they will finally get it: the fundamental commitment to preserve the inherent worth and dignity of every being—every being.

It is time we claim our power and courageously and publicly ask questions that we have been too afraid or too polite to ask. New answers to old questions will *not* save us.

There is no time to be spinning around ourselves saying, "We're so small. Our membership numbers are staying the same!" No kidding—

no one wants to be a part of a country club religion. Who else here is tired of religions that are internally focused and preoccupied with matters that are inherently irrelevant? "Where's my coffee? And why are those curtains crooked, and can you believe he wore that, and do you know what she said, that she said that she did, what he said he would do, but didn't do? And where's my Splenda?"

Preoccupations with idle chatter are a kind of self-poisoning. I think we should excommunicate such petty banter. I think we should teach ourselves how to get out of the committee and into the streets!

It is time that we become a part of a progressive, visionary path that liberates future generations from the theological labyrinth of despair. We want sermons that will wake us up, that will challenge us, that won't put us to sleep week after week. We want to wrestle with the moral issues of our time.

We have to stop asking, "What happens when we die?" because nobody really knows. The real question is, "What happens when we stop living?" The stoicism we face on a daily basis is a symptom of a larger illness called a dulled life. Our lives can be hypnotized by the monotonous commutes, multiplied by the flickering florescent light that falls upon the micromanaging boss who thinks everything you do in your cubicle is an extension of his or her power. Who here is dying a slow and numbing death?

There's no time to be lulled by monotony. There is no time to be blaming other people for our own feelings. If you don't like it, change it. There's no time for crying, or complaining, or gossiping, or clinging to that fashionable grudge bag. No, it is now time to wake up, to rise up, and to carry ourselves into a day worth living.

Let's live one day—this day—with passion and a sense of collective synergy. Let's live one day—this day—by asking questions that really challenge us and make us feel alive. For God's sake, save us from being lulled by complacent theology. For Darwin's sake, save us from being lulled by calcified morality.

Let's flip it. Let's flip it all—the disengagement, the self-preoccupations. As Mark Belletini reminds us:

> *Let's set it all down, you and me.*
> *The disappointments.*
> *Little and large.*
> *The frustrations.*
> *Let's open our fists and drop them.*
> *The useless waiting.*
> *The obsession with what we cannot have.*

The focus on foolish things.
The pin-wheeling worry which wears us out.
The fretting.
Let's throw them down.
The comparisons of ourselves with others.
The competition, as if Domination
was the best name we could give to God.
The cynical assumptions.
The unspoken, shelved anger.
Let's toss them.
The inarticulate suspicions.
The self-doubt.
The pre-emptive self-dumping.
The numbing bouts of self-pity.
Let's sink them all like stones.
Like stones in the pool of this gift of silence.
Let's drop them like hot rocks
into the cool silence.
And when they're gone,
let's lay back gently, and float,
float on the calm surface of the silence.
Let's be supported in this still cradle
of the world, new-born, ready for anything.[2]

Our world can be made new. Our world can be saved time and time again, if, out of this silence, we have the courage to go out into the streets and into our hearts to ask new questions. In doing so, we, as interdependent and limited beings, take up the challenge to create either heaven or hell on Earth—here, now. The choice is ours.

"Is Liberal Religion a Saving Faith?" became a type of wake-up sermon for the congregation and my vocation. It came at an incredibly formative time in my ministry and at an important time in the community's development.

This sermon helped me enter an era in which I was no longer caged by the previous countdown—"thirty-one more sermons… twenty-six more sermons." I stopped taking for granted the privilege of preaching. I eventually became liberated by the invitation to be present and to preach as if it were my last. I found the courage to ask, "What if this really were to be my last service with these people—these beautiful and troubled and complicated people?" This chant helped me break through an initial fear, only to experience a renewed sense of purpose. Rather than being strung out on frenetic adrenaline, I softened into the fierceness of the moment. The urgency I found was not in the need to be somewhere else but to be present. It was as if I had finally stopped counting the prayer beads to feel, for the first time, the essence of that single wooden sphere. Time felt spacious. I was emboldened. Urgency became not an act of desperation but a declaration of hard-earned joy.

I am not speaking of the sentimental. Nor am I speaking of the hollow promise of liberalism-light: "I'm OK. You're OK. We're all OK." Poppycock! True joy is not an extension of such untruths. Joy does not entail talking nice and looking pretty. The essence of joy, compounded by the urgency of now, is a raw, gritty, unadulterated delight. It reveals that where there is suffering, there is responsibility, and where there is duty, there is *power* longing for *compassion*—*might* compelled by *morality,* and *strength* emboldened by *sight.*

Certainly, the preachers at the Poverty Truth Commission and William Furness and Martin Luther King Jr. did not have the privilege of procrastination. They did not have time to whine about not knowing what to say. Their worlds were being torn open. They made pulpits the gateways into moral challenges.

Then it hit me. The elite can be lulled by regularity, wallowing in counterfeit complications—First World problems that pale in comparison to the utter suffering people and animals confront daily. How is it that those sheltered from suffering claim the right to be fatigued by routine? Meanwhile, those crippled by life—*standing bare, naked, and dejected*—would die to have the chance to regularly tell their stories, to proclaim their vision of a world made whole. Imagine the risk required to give voice to the acute torment of these afflictions. Seeing the pulpit through the eyes of the dejected inspired me to preach or die.

The death that I am speaking of is far more damming than becoming a bloodless corpse. I am now far more willing to accept death than to preach without purpose. I am tired of being fatigued by being a victim of affluence. I would rather be so damn exhausted from fighting and struggling and breaking through walls of *bleached bones* than face the graffiti on the walls that read, "Too late."

These two words have been imprinted on my corneas. Daily, these words continually exorcise me from complacency, calling me to preach or die.

3

Democratize the Pulpit

❖ ❖ ❖ Dare to poll the members and visitors of the congregation about issues that matter to them. From the perspective of those in the pews, what are the moral issues of the time? What are congregants struggling with publicly and personally? When democratizing the pulpit, the concerns of the people can be used to brush off the liturgical dust and cleanse the sanctuary of spectators while filling the pews with stakeholders. ❖

In Unitarian Universalism, there is no higher authority than the gathered members. An illustration of that authority is the process by which congregations find their settled (permanent) ministers. In my case, when the congregation's search committee selected me as its final candidate, I spent nine days meeting with and being interviewed by members of the congregation. I preached twice, and then the congregation held a formal meeting and voted. We agreed earlier that if there were anything less than 90 percent approval, then we would not enter into a ministerial partnership together. Thankfully, all but one member voted in favor of my appointment and, in doing so, the gathered members called me to the historic pulpit of the First Unitarian Church of Philadelphia.

All Unitarian Universalist congregations consider their pulpits to be the *free pulpit*—where the preacher has the privilege of freedom of speech. In our tradition, a minister cannot be disciplined or fired for delivering a message that is contrary to the views of the membership. No church leader, no denominational body, and no legal agency have the authority to expurgate a settled minister from a *free pulpit* for the content he or she speaks from it. This is made possible by the vote of the gathered members. Their vote endows the preacher with one of the few places in the world where both *free speech* and *free exercise of religion* are unequivocally protected. The privilege of preaching from a *free pulpit* comes with profound responsibility. It is a power that I have come to believe is emboldened when shared.

In my fifth year of consecutively preaching for this same congregation, I found myself doubting why members of the church would want to come to my worship services. I experienced a profound and prolonged insecurity, and even doubted why members were routinely giving me high marks in preaching and worship. My doubts originated from feeling that I would be unable to produce good work in the future because I felt I had run out of things to say. I found myself having the impulse to recycle ideas that I had previously shared. I needed a wake-up call, which is why I turned to those who had granted me access to the free pulpit.

I used social networking media and various forms of paper communication to invite members and visitors to send me lists of the moral issues of our time. There were two stipulations: first, their response had to be written in the form of a question; and second, it had to be short enough to fit on the kiosk on the front of the church. Dozens and dozens of questions began pouring in—topics I would have never considered or have had the courage to preach.

I narrowed down the submissions to the top forty-three topics that I was genuinely interested in and challenged to preach. I then returned the list to members and friends of the church and asked them to vote on which questions they found to be compelling, interesting, neutral, or uninteresting to them. (I later realized that "compelling" and "interesting" were too close in meaning.) The results of the survey were just as fascinating as were the original submissions. Table 3.1 reprints the survey, and Table 3.2 tallies the responses. (Note that not all people responded to every question.) Table 3.3, using an average generated by assigning each type of response a numerical value (compelling=1, interesting=2, neutral=3, not interested=4) presents the averages in order of level of interest suggested from the responses.

This survey was conducted in the spring of 2011. Interestingly, the question—"What's the Future of Catholicism?"—received the most "not interested" votes. Two years later, after Pope Benedict resigned, this question was dominating the world. I chose not to preach on this topic in 2011 because of a lack of interest, but when that changed, I knew exactly what question to explore on Easter 2013.

Some may be surprised to see that "Is Public Education a Public Responsibility?" was the highest rated question. This is not normally a widely sought-after preaching subject, but it was for us. Why? Two years earlier, the congregation undertook a democratic process to select a single social justice theme. "Education and Literacy" received twice as many votes as did any other social justice topic. This happened because a young man, who had moved to Philadelphia from Pittsburg to start his teaching career, gave an impassioned cry for help. While underneath the portrait of William Furness, he spoke about how the public school system was caught in epic funding battles and the most needy were often the most neglected. He informed us that 1 out of 5 adults in Philadelphia could not read—a claim he supported with the data that 22 percent of adults in Philadelphia could not fill out a job application. I heard others make the point that Unitarian Universalists were the third most educated of any religious group in the United States. The Pew Forum on Religion and Public Life reported in 2008 that "over 74% of Hindus, 59% of Jews and 51% of Unitarians have 4 or more years of college, compared with 27% of the total population."[3] This led one member to ask, "What will we do with our privilege?" Small groups started to make connections between illiteracy and some of the other theme options: racism and poverty. Coalitions began to organically form and, to our amazement, the congregation became more focused than ever.

Members of the church adopted a local public school, built a library from scratch, and trained and organized a corps of volunteers to serve as reading buddies for students most weekdays. Well over two-thirds of the members of the church participated in some activity related to the literacy projects over a three-year period. This explains why this particular subject was so important: members were already stakeholders in the public education system.

The media regularly reported on these activities. I think it was because many religious groups had been advocating for public funds for private schools, creating the false image that all religions are against public schools. Members in our religious community inspired us to take shared responsibility for the health and vitality of our neighborhoods and to work together to strengthen our public schools. Our stance was, apparently, newsworthy. Therefore, the answer to the sermon question—"Are Public Schools a Public Responsibility?"—had already been lived in the deeds of those dedicated people in the pews.

Another interesting question that mobilized people to action was "Is Your Health My Problem?" Leaders in the congregation had recently organized a healthcare debate with members of the U.S. Congress and representatives of the Pennsylvania General Assembly. The congregants collaborated with local health advocacy groups, and the church served as a regional community center through which voters organized. As a result, the sermon topic was intimately connected to the skillful leadership of a number of effective leaders. I was proud that what was happening on a Sunday morning complemented the community's rallying cries for access to affordable healthcare. It felt like we were truly engaging in the moral issues of our time.

Given the social justice sentiments of the congregation, I was surprised that "Should Prisons Be Privatized?" did not end up higher on the list. A year later, Lee Paczulla, our field education student from Harvard Divinity School, offered a series of adult religious education programs and sermons on this topic. She drew from Michelle Alexander's must-read book *The New Jim Crow: Mass Incarceration in the Age of Colorblindness*. Thanks to Lee's efforts, the congregation spent the next four years undertaking advocacy work on the topic of prison reform.

I understood why some of the other topics received low ratings. Many people did not know the meaning of Blue laws or even see their contemporary relevance. The "Why Are Atheists So Sexy?" seemed odd. And we had already explored the subject of vengeance when discussing the ethics of the Iraq War and Guantanamo. Besides, the answer to the question about vengeance was self-evident. Also, the immortality question showed low interest because it is not one that captivates Unitarian Universalists, with their focus on the here and now.

The results of the ritual circumcision question surprised me the most. I found it peculiar that a religious community so dedicated to issues of sexual ethics and children's rights was not compelled to explore the ethics of ritual circumcision—a subject that has since been getting more media attention because of domestic and international policy battles. The subject compelled only nine respondents, whereas twice as many were repelled by it, and a supermajority of the respondents were neutral (indifferent?) to the subject. I wondered whether it would have received a higher rating if the sermon was about religious-based genital alterations on girls. Although these subjects are violent and disturbing, Unitarian Universalists do not shy away from controversial or complicated justice issues. Why then would ritual circumcision receive such a low rating?

Even though the democratic process revealed that the subject of circumcision was unpopular, I was compelled by the members' vote of no confidence to take to the *free pulpit*. Ritual-based genital alterations on children are, indeed, one of the most charged ethical/religious questions of our time. It is a subject that many religious professionals avoid. It rarely receives public attention, and if it does, the subject is shut down for fear of being perceived as anti-Semitic. It is a third-rail in religious ethics and American politics. I was curious why Unitarian Universalists, who are not afraid to talk about sex, war, torture, gender, or religion and politics, would shy away from this topic. This was another compelling outcome from this democratization process.

Another interesting result was the fact that my service about circumcision received, by far, the lowest worship attendance of the entire year; however, when I later presented a paper on this topic at the American Political Science Association, my research was one of the highest downloaded papers on the Social Science Research Network. And yet in our church, there was less than half of our normal attendance. There were no storms that day, no parades or holidays to blame. Despite the fact that this sermon did not inspire participation, I believed it to be a very important topic. For that reason, we coupled the worship service with a film showing of *Cut: Slicing Through the Myths of Circumcision*. We invited the filmmaker Eliyahu Ungar-Sargon to speak after the event, attended by two dozen people, mostly from outside of the congregation. In the end, I am proud that I had the courage to take on the subject. I am also pleased that my further treatment of the subject was also featured at an international children's rights conference in the United Kingdom and a legal conference sponsored by the Law and Society Association.

Another way to make sense of these results is to say that my interests have not always been in alignment with my community's. The *free pulpit* makes this disagreement possible, and even necessary, in order to engage in the moral and intellectual development of the people and the preacher. Persuasion from those in the pews is another, equally significant tool for engaging the congregation in the moral issues of our time. As seen with literacy and prison reform, it often takes a few passionate, dedicated people to inspire members to get out of the committee and into the streets. This is the ultimate goal of a democratized congregation.

❖

The model of democratizing the pulpit not only invited people to help choose the sermon topics but also invited them to participate in co-creating the worship services. I was thrilled to discover that twenty-eight people accepted the invitation to serve as worship associates. Half of them had never helped create worship before. The survey proved effective in helping increase participation in the worship arts program. I felt supported. Most importantly, I found my passion for preaching again.

That next year, I always had at least one volunteer to assist me with the service, and often there were two associates per service, sometimes three. This process helped us bolster participation. In fact, four of the survey respondents said they were not members of the congregation but wanted to help with specific services. They eventually served as worship associates, and within a year, three of the four had joined the church. Who would have thought that a survey posted on Facebook about sermon themes would create a gateway to membership? I wonder if this result would be replicable in other congregations.

Twenty-six people completed the final question in the survey, which was an open-ended textbox, inviting respondents to share their comments. A majority of the respondents expressed gratitude and support, such as "Great list!" and "Keep up the great work!" and "Looking forward to another year of amazing worship!" Other comments included helpful suggestions such as "Some of these topics seem ripe for a point/counterpoint," and, "How about a sermon about when and why idealism fails?" I was intrigued that many of the comments were actual responses to the sermon questions, which led to several pastoral encounters.

One respondent said, "If I could put a number on the 'compelling' column, Ethical Eating would be #1. After thinking about this issue for a number of years, I now believe how we treat other species (especially the factory farm-raised ones) is a form of slavery. I wonder if this comparison could help to awaken consciences." I later shared a vegan meal with this respondent, and I said that I thought that the comparison was counterproductive. He agreed that equating an animal eater to a slave owner is not honest or persuasive, and I reminded him that persuasion was his ultimate goal. I asked him what purpose it served to put people on the defensive. We talked about ways to exercise good judgment and to take a stand without being condescending. We talked about how none of us are exempt from benefiting from unethical food systems.

I told him, "It's not about who is right, but about what is right."

He replied, "I get it. I do not have to spend all my energy pointing out who is wrong."

"Yes," I answered. "That's because, at some level, we all have blood on our hands."

Gentle persuasion, thus, became the theme of our conversation, and later a sermon title.

Another respondent reflected upon the question "To Be or Not To Be?" She asked, "Is this sermon about suicide? If so, I am not interested in helping with the worship service, but I am interested in talking with you." Although I saw her in worship before, we had never really connected. I called her cell phone. Two days later, she was in my office pulling away her long sleeves to reveal the scars on her wrists. She had gained some emotional distance from being suicidal the year before and offered me a series of concrete ideas to include in my sermon. The most poignant was the realization that she was not her past. She came to self-differentiate between those things that had once crippled her. They had less power over her now because she came to see that those troubles are now over. Given that this woman had only attended two worship services and had not attended in over a year, I am not certain that she would have contacted me had it not been for the survey. Who would have thought that a survey about worship would result in a pathway to pastoral care?

Ultimately, the survey is about being in relationship with people—one of the most powerful byproducts of democratizing the pulpit. It served as an invitation to start a conversation, to begin a collaborative process, and to treat every person as a worthy stakeholder in our worship services.

One respondent summarized it nicely: "This seems to me to be a wise use of the democratic process because it allows diversity to flourish. If you had used this process to choose a single theme for the whole season, it would not be a good thing." He went on to clarify, "I am very sensitive to authority issues and…I think voting works best when it results in the expression of diversity and not when it works toward the 'tyranny of the majority.'" He closed by saying, "By the way, I hope 'Doubt as a Religious Practice' makes the cut. I can't wait for that sermon." As noted in Table 3.2, the "Are

You Sure?" sermon was the only one with zero people responding "not interested." I delivered it as the Easter service in 2012, one of the most attended of the year.

In addition to revitalizing worship, recruiting members, and engaging in pastoral care, there was another byproduct of the survey: increased attendance. Our church's communications director created a postcard of the worship schedule with the sermon titles. Apparently, some people used it to schedule their participation. Others used our social networking website to RSVP to the worship services and to share the blurbs with their friends. Those who participated in the survey told me they felt responsible for helping to get the word out. Some people felt proud that the sermon questions they proposed made it to my initial list and were affirmed by the democratic process. One congregant asked me to move one sermon to the weekend her parents were going to be in town. Apparently, the sermon "How Do You Love Someone Seemingly Unlovable?" had become a hotly debated topic at their dinner table. After thanking me for the service, her parents told me that the entire family had been anticipating this talk—the subject of which I will discuss in chapter 7.

By democratizing the pulpit, ultimately worshipers changed roles. The congregants moved from spectators to liturgical stakeholders. My role changed, too. I was no longer a lone sermonizer, buried in books. I was engaged in extraordinary conversations with a wide variety of people. They shared with me sources that I would have never been exposed to otherwise. Preaching became a less lonely process, and the product became a personal exchange from one investor in the community to another. Those who participated invested not only in learning how to be effective responders to oppressive agendas, but also, together, we were learning to be the ethical agenda setters of our time.

TABLE 3.1.: SURVEY QUESTIONS FOR DEMOCRATIZING THE PULPIT 2011–2012

Sermons for September 2011–June 2012. Reverend Nate invited members to submit questions to serve as possible sermon topics. He received over 100 suggestions. He thought about which topics compelled and challenged him. He then narrowed it down to the following forty-three sermon titles. You can help him narrow these even further by completing the following survey. The top thirty titles will become the subjects for his sermons during the September 2011 to June 2012 church year. This collaborative process is undertaken in honor of the Unitarian Universalist principle that reads, "We affirm and promote the right of conscience and the use of the democratic process within our congregations and in society at large."

Question 1.a. Full name   **Question 1.b.** E-mail address

Question 2. Please rate each possible topic using one of the following options: *compelling, interesting, neutral,* or *not interested.* Meaning, which of the sermons titles would catch your attention if you read it on the church kiosk?

1. Are Sex and Religion Compatible?
2. Are You Accommodating or a Doormat?
3. Are You Sure? (Doubt as Spiritual Practice)
4. Can Justice Be Blind?
5. Can Morality Be Objective?
6. Can We Really Move This Place?
7. Can We Talk Trash? (Children Raised in Landfills)
8. Come on Philly, Where's the Love?
9. Do You Have the Right to Die?
10. Do You Want To Be Immortal?
11. Does Acceptance Come with Age?
12. Elite—Who? Us?
13. How Do You Love Someone Seemingly Unlovable?
14. How Much Should We Take? (Distributive Justice)
15. Is "Free Will" an Illusion?
16. Is Abstinence-Only Education Moral?
17. Is American Exceptionalism a Sin?
18. Is Ritual Circumcision Ethical?
19. Is Intelligence a Gift or Foe?
20. Is Public Education a Public Responsibility?
21. Is Self-Acceptance Possible?
22. Is the "Silent Treatment" Effective?
23. Is Vengeance a Virtue?
24. Is Your Health My Problem?
25. Kindness—Idealistic or Realistic?

26. Purchasing Power—Does It Matter?
27. Should Blue Laws Be Overturned?
28. Should Prisons Be Privatized?
29. Should We Become a Bilingual Nation?
30. To Be or Not To Be?
31. What Have We Learned Since 9/11?
32. What Makes You Keep on Living?
33. What Unites the Religious Right and the Liberal Left?
34. What's a "Good Death"?
35. What's Ethical about Eating?
36. What's the Future of Catholicism?
37. What's the Line Between Pride and Arrogance?
38. Whose God Rules? (Religion and Politics)
39. Why Are Atheists So Sexy?
40. Why Are Judgments Like Boomerangs?
41. Why Cross Borders? (Immigration)
42. Why Do So Few Religions Proselytize?
43. Why Is Life So Beautiful?

Question 3. Are you interested in serving as a worship associate and helping plan and co-lead any of these services? If so, which ones? A worship associate meets with Reverend Nate two weeks before the service to brainstorm the topic and then the Thursday night before to run through the service in full. He believes in the collaborative process and looks forward to your participation in co-creating meaningful worship.

Question 4. Any questions or comments to share with Reverend Nate?

Notes: The following survey was conducted using Survey Monkey.

TABLE 3.2. RESPONSES TO SURVEY QUESTIONS TO DEMOCRATIZE THE PULPIT 2011–2012

Questions	Compelling	Interesting	Neutral	Not Interested	Rating Average	Response Count
Are Sex and Religion Compatible?	23.9% (16)	35.8% (24)	28.4% (19)	11.9% (8)	2.28	67
Are You Accommodating or a Doormat?	24.6% (17)	34.8% (24)	27.5% (19)	13.0% (9)	2.29	69
Are You Sure? (Doubt as Spiritual Practice)	40.6% (28)	46.4% (32)	13.0% (9)	0.0% (0)	1.72	69
Can Justice Be Blind?	30.3% (20)	42.4% (28)	22.7% (15)	4.5% (3)	2.02	66
Can Morality Be Objective?	34.8% (24)	34.8% (24)	26.1% (18)	4.3% (3)	2.00	69
Can We Really Move This Place?	22.7% (15)	25.8% (17)	40.9% (27)	10.6% (7)	2.39	66
Can We Talk Trash? (Children Raised in Landfills)	27.9% (19)	38.2% (26)	22.1% (15)	11.8% (8)	2.18	68
Come on Philly, Where's the Love?	41.2% (28)	22.1% (15)	27.9% (19)	8.8% (6)	2.04	68
Do You Have the Right to Die?	37.9% (25)	43.9% (29)	10.6% (7)	7.6% (5)	1.88	66
Do You Want To Be Immortal?	11.9% (8)	35.8% (24)	26.9% (18)	25.4% (17)	2.66	67
Does Acceptance Come with Age?	19.1% (13)	44.1% (30)	30.9% (21)	5.9% (4)	2.24	68
Elite—Who? Us?	35.8% (24)	41.8% (28)	13.4% (9)	9.0% (6)	1.96	67
How Do You Love Someone Seemingly Unlovable?	46.4% (32)	34.8% (24)	15.9% (11)	2.9% (2)	1.75	69
How Much Should We Take? (Distributive Justice)	41.5% (27)	38.5% (25)	15.4% (10)	4.6% (3)	1.83	65
Is "Free Will" an Illusion?	40.6% (28)	24.6% (17)	24.6% (17)	10.1% (7)	2.04	69
Is Abstinence-Only Education Moral?	19.7% (13)	28.8 (19)	31.8% (21)	19.7% (13)	2.52	66
Is American Exceptionalism a Sin?	14.9% (10)	41.8% (28)	34.3% (23)	9.0% (6)	2.37	67
Is Ritual Circumcision Ethical?	13.0% (9)	27.5% (19)	33.3% (23)	26.1% (18)	2.72	69

Questions	Compelling	Interesting	Neutral	Not Interested	Rating Average	Response Count
Is Intelligence a Gift or Foe?	23.1% (15)	33.8% (22)	30.8% (20)	12.3% (8)	2.23	65
Is Public Education a Public Responsibility?	45.6% (31)	41.2% (28)	10.3% (7)	2.9% (2)	1.71	68
Is Self-Acceptance Possible?	40.0% (28)	42.9% (30)	11.4% (8)	5.7% (4)	1.83	70
Is the "Silent Treatment" Effective?	9.0% (6)	32.8% (22)	43.3% (29)	14.9% (10)	2.64	67
Is Vengeance a Virtue?	13.4% (9)	28.4% (19)	37.3% (25)	20.9% (14)	2.66	67
Is Your Health My Problem?	37.3% (25)	43.3% (29)	14.9% (10)	4.5% (3)	1.87	67
Kindness—Idealistic or Realistic?	37.7% (26)	42.0% (29)	15.9% (11)	4.3% (3)	1.87	69
Purchasing Power—Does It Matter?	26.5% (18)	30.9% (21)	36.8% (25)	5.9% (4)	2.22	68
Should Blue Laws Be Overturned?	6.0% (4)	23.9% (16)	35.8% (24)	34.3% (23)	2.99	67
Should Prisons Be Privatized?	11.9% (8)	38.8% (26)	31.3% (21)	17.9% (12)	2.55	67
Should We Become a Bilingual Nation?	19.1% (13)	41.2% (28)	29.4% (20)	10.3% (7)	2.31	68
To Be or Not To Be?	14.7% (10)	23.5% (16)	42.6% (29)	19.1% (13)	2.66	68
What Have We Learned Since 9/11?	34.3% (23)	31.3% (21)	26.9% (18)	7.5% (5)	2.07	67
What Makes You Keep on Living?	45.1% (32)	33.8% (24)	16.9% (12)	4.2% (3)	1.80	71
What Unites the Religious Right and the Liberal Left?	40.6% (28)	40.6% (28)	15.9% (11)	2.9% (2)	1.81	69
What's a "Good Death"?	47.1% (32)	32.4% (22)	16.2% (11)	4.4% (3)	1.78	68
What's Ethical about Eating?	34.3% (23)	29.9% (20)	22.4% (15)	13.4% (9)	2.15	67
What's the Future of Catholicism?	14.9% (10)	19.4% (13)	25.4% (17)	40.3% (27)	2.91	67
What's the Line between Pride and Arrogance?	31.9% (22)	24.6% (17)	37.7% (26)	5.8% (4)	2.17	69

Questions	Compelling	Interesting	Neutral	Not Interested	Rating Average	Response Count
Whose God Rules? (Religion and Politics)	34.3% (23)	32.8% (22)	26.9% (18)	6.0% (4)	2.04	67
Why Are Atheists So Sexy?	13.4% (9)	31.3% (21)	26.9% (18)	28.4% (19)	2.70	67
Why Are Judgments Like Boomerangs?	27.1% (19)	37.1% (26)	27.1% (19)	8.6% (6)	2.17	70
Why Cross Borders? (Immigration)	26.1% (18)	46.4% (32)	24.6% (17)	2.9% (2)	2.04	69
Why Do So Few Religions Proselytize?	26.5% (18)	36.8% (25)	27.9% (19)	8.8% (6)	2.19	68
Why Is Life So Beautiful?	44.8% (30)	25.4% (17)	23.9% (16)	6.0% (4)	1.91	67

Number of Respondents 71

TABLE 3.3. RATING AVERAGES

Sermon Questions	Rating Average
Is Public Education a Public Responsibility?	1.71
Are You Sure? (Doubt as Spiritual Practice)	1.72
How Do You Love Someone Seemingly Unlovable?	1.75
What's a "Good Death"?	1.78
What Makes You Keep on Living?	1.80
What Unites the Religious Right and the Liberal Left?	1.81
How Much Should We Take? (Distributive Justice)	1.83
Is Self-Acceptance Possible?	1.83
Is Your Health My Problem?	1.87
Kindness—Idealistic or Realistic?	1.87
Do You Have the Right to Die?	1.88
Why Is Life So Beautiful?	1.91
Elite—Who? Us?	1.96
Can Morality Be Objective?	2.00
Can Justice Be Blind?	2.02
Come on Philly, Where's the Love?	2.04
Is "Free Will" an Illusion?	2.04
Whose God Rules? (Religion and Politics)	2.04
Why Cross Borders? (Immigration)	2.04
What Have We Learned Since 9/11?	2.07
What's Ethical about Eating?	2.15
What's the Line Between Pride and Arrogance?	2.17
Why Are Judgments Like Boomerangs?	2.17
Can We Talk Trash (Children Raised in Landfills)	2.18
Why Do So Few Religions Proselytize?	2.19
Purchasing Power—Does It Matter?	2.22
Is Intelligence a Gift or Foe?	2.23
Does Acceptance Come with Age?	2.24
Are Sex and Religion Compatible?	2.28
Are You Accommodating or a Doormat?	2.29
Should We Become a Bilingual Nation?	2.31
Is American Exceptionalism a Sin?	2.37
Can We Really Move This Place?	2.39

Is Abstinence-Only Education Moral?	2.52
Should Prisons Be Privatized?	2.55
Is the "Silent Treatment" Effective?	2.64
Do You Want To Be Immortal?	2.66
Is Vengeance a Virtue?	2.66
To Be or Not To Be?	2.66
Why Are Atheists So Sexy?	2.70
Is Ritual Circumcision Ethical?	2.72
What's the Future of Catholicism?	2.91
Should Blue Laws Be Overturned?	2.99

4

Preempt Procrastination

❖ ❖ ❖ Spiritual practices, such as preaching, require discipline.
My discipline comes from trying to meet a series of
milestones. I meet with worship associates (congregants or
colleagues) to brainstorm the content, sources, and form of
a sermon at least ten days before I deliver it. Then I present
a complete worship script and fully drafted sermon to my
worship associate(s) at least three days before I preach it. After
that (or at the same time) I invite Internet friends to review
the sermon. Finally, the next morning, I revise the text, then
rest; on the preaching day, I revive the content for worship.
My working formula is simple: review, revise, rest, and revive.
By employing professional time-management disciplines,
preachers will be free to spend more time with family and
to get a full night's rest. Imagine spending a lifetime sleeping
every night before preaching! ❖

In my first year of full-time preaching, I lived on a church
campus in a parsonage of the Unitarian Church of Staten Island,
New York. I spent nearly every Saturday night working on my
sermon, often until 2 a.m. or later. I slept a few hours, showered,
and let the adrenaline pump through my fatigued body. Physically,
my hands sometimes shook. Mentally, I struggled to concentrate,
and my memory of the day became blurred. I barreled through the
Sunday morning experience only to rush back to the parsonage.
By mid-afternoon, I was sprawled out on the couch taking an epic

nap. I would wake up a few hours later, order food, and try to get to bed before midnight, but I would often awake in the middle of the night not knowing which time zone I was in. My day off was spent recovering, and I repeated this pattern week after week.

Many clergy joke about endless night-before sermon writing. We reinforce for one another the addiction of late-night writing by making light of the profession. We justify the process by saying things like, "I work better under pressure," and, "I'm most creative past midnight." I became enveloped in this culture while in seminary, and it was fortified during my field education and internship years. During this formative time, I noticed that families of clergy also accepted this culture. I met a number of adult PKs (preacher kids) who said, "Yeah, my father always wrote his sermons the night before," and, "We knew to get out of the house on Saturday nights." From the personal to the professional, these interlocking cultures reinforced a harmful process.

I ended my first year of congregational ministry utterly exhausted. Intellectually, I knew this was not sustainable, but, habitually, the trait had already become embedded in my DNA. It felt similar to what addicts describe as going through withdrawal—even though we know it is bad for us, we cannot stop.

The purpose of this chapter is to explain how I exorcised from my life sleepless Saturday nights. My hope is that the ideas presented here will help my colleagues and their families and their religious communities create a counterculture based on mutuality, professionalism, and self-care. In doing so, we can attribute our recovery to two factors: *effective time management* within a *culture of support*. Both are required if clergy are to succeed.

After I finished the consultant contract in Staten Island, I moved to Philadelphia to begin my first settlement. I knew I wanted to make some changes in my preaching process but feared I would revert to unhealthy habits. Thankfully, the leaders at the First Unitarian Church had created a robust worship arts program in which one to two worship associates were available to me each week. At our first worship retreat, they taught me about best practices for creating good products, and I expressed my intention to create a healthy process. Concretely, I proposed a draft of a preaching schedule stating when I would be researching and writing along with when they could join me to brainstorm and rehearse the sermon. This plan was not that terribly farfetched because they already had instituted a culture of supporting preachers. Worship associates were delighted to be a part of the process and contributed greatly to the quality of our products. Over the years, we developed a habit of scheduling our weeks as follows. (See Tables 4.1. and 4.2.) This time-management strategy is based on the understanding that it takes approximately twenty hours a week to research, write, rehearse, perform, and evaluate a worship service.

Structure can offer us freedom. For me, this method of preempting procrastination liberated me from the harmful habits I had developed in my first year of serving as the solo minister of a church. Rather than being pressured by the high stakes of Sunday morning, I scheduled low-stakes meetings with caring, supportive people who held me accountable. We met to brainstorm the scope of the service, to choose readings, and to determine a form that could be used to deliver the content. (See chapter 7 on methods for choosing a sermon form.) This allowed me the chance to verbally process with another person and let me start writing based on a clear outline. The rehearsal gave the worship associates and me time to connect with one another and to engage in our own moral, intellectual, and faith development. By asking external reviewers to comment on the sermon, I added one more step in quality control. These weekly milestones freed me to leave Saturday days for rites of passage and pastoral care and Saturday nights for quality time with my family. Sleeping well on Saturday nights became one of my most coveted times to practice self-care. Self-care, I learned, must be a preemptive act, not simply a reaction to fatigue or conflict. These steps freed me to be truly present in worship, to bring a kind of energy and joy to the experience that I would not have been physically able to do if adrenaline and caffeine were my only fuel. I have come to experience how this structure gave me freedom.

As mentioned previously, I do not expect other preachers to adopt my own exorcisms, but my hope is that others will conduct their own. The following formula may be of use to preachers in developing their own exorcises. I will use my sermon about Leo Frank (Appendix B) to illustrate how I attempted to put this preaching theory into practice.

In 2013, the church's theater discussion group (similar to a book club) asked me to preach on *Parade*, a Tony Award-winning book and musical score. The musical dramatized the 1913 trial of

Leo Frank, a Jewish factory manager from New York who was accused, tried, and sentenced to death for raping and murdering a thirteen-year-old employee in Atlanta, Georgia. Instead of capital punishment, the governor of Georgia commuted his death sentence to life in prison. In outrage, statesmen and citizens formed a lynching party, kidnapped Leo Frank in the middle of the night, and hanged him from an oak tree near the girl's home. Thousands of people watched his body being paraded through Atlanta. No legal action was taken against the members of the lynching party. This event sparked the revival of the Ku Klux Klan in Georgia as well as the formation of the national Anti-Defamation League. *Parade* served as the source text for our worship service about the one-hundred-year anniversary of the lynching of Leo Frank.

Step 1. Brainstorm

On a Thursday afternoon, ten days before I was scheduled to preach on the musical *Parade,* I worked with my music director to draft a worship script, complete with an opening reading, hymns, and other musical selections. We also organized musicians from the play to perform at the upcoming service. I then rushed off to an off-site wedding rehearsal before returning to the church in time to rehearse the sermon scheduled for three days later.

The brainstorming session for the sermon about Parade did not happen on that Thursday night. Rather, the worship associate and I attended a Saturday matinee performance of *Parade,* eight days before the service. We watched the musical and afterward spent twenty minutes in the lobby talking about the disturbing nature of the story and the magnificent performances. Our discussion went from talking about Leo Frank's case to analyzing the lyrics to a pastoral exchange. We began to reflect on the worship associate's Jewish upbringing. Our multilayered conversation was cut off because the alarm I set on my phone went off. I used it as a reminder that I had limited time to get across town to meet my friends for an early dinner. I wanted to give myself time to walk there so that, in addition to the interpersonal time with the associate, I would also have introspective time to contemplate the play and our conversation.

The following Sunday morning, I preached a sermon I had finished preparing a few days earlier. The service went well, and I had meetings that afternoon and saw a movie with my partner that night. I rested on Monday morning. That afternoon, I answered e-mails and prepared to teach an adult religious education class that evening on religion in America. Tuesdays are normally my day off, but this week, I spent the afternoon conducting a memorial service. That night, I spent some downtime at home.

Step 2. Write

I spent Wednesday researching the Leo Frank case in between answering e-mails and holding a supervisory session with a field education student, followed by a meeting with a new board member, then a session with my therapist. My time with the seminarian was spent doing theological reflection on her forthcoming children's program about Esther, the Jewish queen of Persia, and the holiday, Purim. I was impressed that she chose to focus on this lesser emphasized story in her curriculum on biblical literacy. My meeting with the new trustee was spent telling the other side of a story of a conflict between a member and a former staff member. The gossip mill in the church had given this new trustee false impressions. This seemed to be a reoccurring theme in my own therapy session. I used the time to work through my emotional reaction to a personal situation and finally admitted that I had spent over a year falsely believing that my opinions were facts. This was an incredibly freeing insight that seemed directly related to the Leo Frank story. The invidiously discriminatory opinions held by residents of Atlanta, not the facts of the case, led a group of public officials and citizens to lynch an innocent man. That night, I stayed up late reading public school curricula about this case while streaming the PBS special *The People v. Leo Frank*.

Step 3. Rehearse

I spent the next day writing content for my sermon in between answering emails, facilitating a staff meeting, and going to the gym to meet my personal trainer. That night, five members of the theater discussion group joined me in the shared ministry suite. Normally, this time would be spent rehearsing the worship service in full, but this week was spent with those who had seen the play. Together, we created a timeline of the case with material from a half-dozen sources, and we had a robust debate about anti-Semitism in America, then and now. We left the meeting not having answered my most pressing question: How do I preach a sermon to three different audiences—those who have never heard about Leo Frank, those who have but did not see the production, and those who recently accepted our invitation to watch the musical?

After everyone had left, my worship associate stayed behind for a few minutes. I shared with him my insecurities: feeling overwhelmed and unfocused by the breadth of the material and confused about how to preach to three audiences. He gave me an inspired pep talk and a pat on the shoulder. Although I did not have a formal rehearsal, I was so familiar with the material that, if needed, I could come up with something. I just needed some time to focus my ideas. Late that night, while trying to sleep, I realized that the problem of preaching to three audiences was an opportunity to determine the sermon form. In the dark, I sketched out a new outline for the sermon, left it on my nightstand, and finally fell asleep.

Step 4. Revise

On Friday morning, I typed a revised outline for the sermon and went into a video conference call regarding an upcoming research project on human rights. My friend then sent a text to me to see whether I was free for lunch, and I accepted. I returned to my office to rewrite my sermon, during which time I received an e-mail from a member of the church informing me that her wife had been admitted to the hospital. I called her and accepted the invitation to visit on Saturday afternoon. During the conversation, I saw from my office window a man who usually sleeps on the steps of our church experience another manic episode. I cut the phone call short to go outside and check on him. Knowing that the children from the church's daycare center were about to be released, I invited him to walk and talk with me, but he refused and yelled profanities and left in a rush. I returned to my office and tried to finish the sermon, aware that in a few hours I had to pick my parents up from the airport.

Step 5. Review

I did not meet my writing goals, which is why after my parents were settled in their hotel on Friday night, I returned to my computer and by 2 a.m. e-mailed a final draft to my worship associate. The next morning, I met my folks for brunch, and we walked around Philadelphia. Then my partner met us for lunch, and my parents joined him to see *Parade*. This gave me a few hours to visit the congregant in the hospital and make final edits on the sermon.

On a good week, I would have posted on Facebook on Friday morning an invitation for people to peer review my sermon. I did not achieve this goal. Thankfully, the worship associate was able to read the sermon on Saturday morning and send me his suggestions. I had an hour to integrate them and to practice speaking aloud my sermon. I finally felt clear and confident.

Step 6. Rest

Saturday evening was family night! We enjoyed talking about the play and spent some real quality time together. I came to the dinner feeling both deeply satisfied with my work and fully capable of giving my full attention to my family. Even though I had ultimately worked 62 hours that week, I did not feel burnt out. I worked hard and tried to use the most of my limited time. I knew it paid off because on Saturday night, I fell into a deep sleep.

Step 7. Revive

On Sunday morning, I awoke with clarity. I came early to the church to putter around the sanctuary. I fiddled with the candles and rearranged the chancel chairs and conducted a sound check. I printed out the scripts and met my worship associate an hour before the service to talk through blocking—the staging cues for where we would stand when. My family members arrived, and I had time to reintroduce my parents to community members. I was fully ready to revive the sermon.

I began by telling the story of Leo Frank solely through the eyes of the statesmen of Atlanta. I tried to be so convincing that for those who had never heard of Leo Frank, they would be persuaded by my seemingly objective account to take the position of the all-white male jury. For those who knew the play and who knew the history of the incident, they would have the content knowledge to see the holes in my arguments, while at the same time, be entertained by this rhetorical device. I then asked members of the congregation to raise their hands if they had never heard of this famous case. Over half of the congregation responded. I explained that if all they knew is what I had told them, then they would find themselves to be sympathetic to members of the KKK that lynched Leo Frank. I proceeded to tell the story through the eyes of Leo Frank and introduced compelling evidence that proved his innocence. Ultimately, I closed the sermon with a reflection on our ability to live as if our limited opinions are facts. I demonstrated the serious problems that arise when our opinions are biased and used to justify causing harm—"Justified" being the title of the sermon.

We can feel so justified in our positions that we fail to see another side of the story. (See Appendix B for the full sermon.)

Afterward, the newly elected trustee asked, "Did you write that sermon for me?" I laughed, and we talked about our appreciation for seeing multiple sides of the conflict occurring between the former staff member and a current church leader. While we were wrapping up the conversation, a parent approached me. She said that while we were in the service, the children had been exploring the book of Esther and learning about a biblical figure she knew nothing about. She expressed her appreciation for a Sunday school that exposed her children to different points of view. That was all I needed to hear to know that we were stimulating one another's moral and intellectual development across the lifespan.

Step 8. Reflect

That next Thursday night was our monthly worship arts meeting. Seven people gathered to talk about the effectiveness of the previous four worship services. When we arrived at the service about Leo Frank, members began a rich discussion about human biases. We read aloud comments that were sent by people who had attended the play who thought the one-sided start to the sermon was particularly effective. One criticized the service for it being such a violent subject, and others appreciated how Leo Frank's tragic story was connected to their own lives, one hundred years later.

I treated these reflection sessions in two different ways. First, I looked for honest and constructive feedback. I shared my own critiques and used the time to verbally set goals for my professional development. Second, I used the time to engage members in their own faith formation. I listened for the sermons they had heard, but I did not preach. I listened for the questions that the sermons evoked in them and how worship helped them grow and learn together. This focus group has served as a monthly way to take the pulse of the congregation: *How is the community? How is worship serving its needs?*

Another way to articulate this process is to use the praxis model of education: reflection, action, action reflected upon. In this context, I worked with a worship associate and members of a theater discussion group to reflect upon the story of Leo Frank. I took action by delivering a sermon designed to use a particular rhetorical form to deliver specific content aimed to reveal a shadow side to the human condition. Together, we reflected upon the worship experience and engaged one another in our own moral and intellectual development. My ultimate purpose was and is to create a culture of learning so that people can use the church as a place to study and grow individually and collectively.

Step 9. Retreat

Once a month, I take a Sunday off from preaching. This allows me the time to do a number of things. Sometimes, I visit the religious education classes that take place simultaneously with the worship service. Other times, I take the whole weekend off and spend it with my family. Quarterly, I use this weekend to engage in some form of professional development.

That particular weekend I went to a conference and flew back on Saturday night. I then attended the service to witness a leader of the church lead worship. She was in a formative time in her life, considering when to apply to seminary. I wanted to be present for her, and I also felt a deep need to be a worshiper, free from the role of worship leader. Her service was one of the most fulfilling religious encounters I had experienced in years. It was deeply refreshing, and I felt honored to be a witness to her profound ministry.

She later told me that the nine-step process that we developed in the church to create worship aided her process. She did a lot of work to prepare her worship service and had a very fruitful rehearsal and editing process. Ultimately, she slept on Saturday night and arrived on Sunday morning feeling engaged and truly present. I am deeply grateful that my previous suffering through endless Saturday nights was not passed to her as a cultural norm. With intentionality and with a good deal of support, our congregation was able to teach her a healthy approach to the craft.

My hope in recounting these details is to make explicit that the method of preempting procrastination, as framed in Tables 4.1. and 4.2., is just that, a method. It is incredibly freeing to put into motion this type of professional time-management technique. However, in practice, I am rarely able to achieve all of these milestones in one given week.

In this particular ten-day period in preparing a sermon about Leo Frank, I was forced to juggle a number of competing needs, both professionally and personally, which is more common than not. Ministry is a complex, relational craft with a great number of predictable responsibilities. Sunday morning always comes and, yet a plethora of unpredictable opportunities to minister also arrive, from memorials and pastoral emergencies, to tending to a manic-depressive neighbor. As clergy members, we know that our time is rarely our own, which is all the more reason to be disciplined with the little time that is under our control.

In the spirit of intellectual honesty, I close this chapter by reiterating several confessions. In a given church year, I have often failed to preschedule my meetings with worship associates. My great theory of meeting with someone ten days before preaching does not always happen. Thankfully, where I fall short, others step up. For instance, the chair of worship arts often connects me with associates and ensures that we have meetings on the shared calendar. This is a helpful way for leaders to hold me accountable to my own goals. When they show up to the brainstorming sessions, I have no choice but to face the low-pressure meeting, which is much less of a problem than being embroiled by the high-pressure Saturday night writing. There are even the weeks when I come to the Thursday rehearsal without a draft sermon, which is far less embarrassing than not having the time to write something of value by Sunday morning. When it comes to writing, I have often felt distracted and tempted to focus on other matters, some important, some not. E-mails and church politics have preoccupied my internal life, diverting me to unhealthy mental habits. On a weekly basis, I typically receive dozens of invitations to procrastinate. The secret, I have found, is to try to preempt reasons to procrastinate while scheduling regular chances to practice self-care, such as physical training, therapy sessions, and time with family. A critical aspect of the art of ministry comes in figuring out how to juggle these competing needs.

Then there are the weeks when I had no other choice but to write the sermon late on a Saturday night. And when those late nights came, and they often did, I had no option but to barrel through the early morning hours determined to preach something valuable. I fell back into the confidence of knowing how to work under pressure, and by 3 a.m. on Sunday morning, I had something worthwhile to present. In those weeks, my process was sloppy, but my product was sufficient and sometimes a success. I had enough experience winging it to know how not to make a fool of myself. I had enough practice to know that when I reached into a magic hat, I would find something to pull out—it was not always a rabbit, but it was always something surprising. In these make-it-happen moments, I did not feel proud, but I did feel relieved. I also felt grateful knowing that I could still perform under pressure. But once I learned to preempt procrastination, I felt freed from the habit of imprisoning myself in the anxiety of regular sleepless Saturday nights. When it happened, it was rare, and therefore I could tolerate the impermanence of this event. I stopped torturing myself with false ideas about the process of preaching—the myth that high-pressure settings magically produced better sermons. On a rare occasion, I found this to be true, but certainly not all the time or even consistently so. I had no other choice but to purge these harmful habits from my preaching process. This exorcism was made possible when my community and I used a low-stakes, relation-based process to help me maintain a sustainable time-management strategy. I was not always able to achieve each milestone, but achieving a majority of them was sufficient. And when the pressures of the week kept me from executing the strategy consistently, I found a way to show up and perform. Sundays come—they always do—whether I am ready or not.

I learned that the pressure of not having time did not exempt me from asking for help. This was made possible when I freed myself from the false notion that sermon writing should be done alone. The craft of preaching is a communal act. Sermons are not born only in solitude. Preaching is a relational craft not done in isolation but co-created in community. A memorable sermon often develops out of suffering, struggle, dialogue, and debate. Sermons are not ad hoc soapbox improvisations. Sermons are professional publications. Every sermon is worthy of peer review, and every preacher is worthy of feedback before going public. Preachers may think they are brilliant in their own minds, but preachers are made brilliant when others taste their half-baked ideas and recommend additional ingredients. Performers know this, journalists know this, researchers know this—professional products require editing, rehearsing, and revising. This is the structure that not only creates high-quality products but also creates a sustainable process. Imagine a truly sustainable preaching schedule.

For me, preaching is similar to self-care: it is a preemptive discipline. The craft requires that I know when to anticipate everyday stressors to ensure they do not imprison me in states of anxiety and restlessness. This kind of structure, which is both strong and flexible, has given me tremendous professional and personal freedom. I wish the same for all my colleagues.

TABLE 4.1. PREACHING MILESTONES	
Step 1. Brainstorm	Determine the scope of topic and sources, and choose the form.
Step 2. Write	Write first draft of worship script and sermon.
Step 3. Rehearse	Practice the worship script and sermon with associate.
Step 4. Revise	Create second draft based on feedback from rehearsal.
Step 5. Review	Send for external review and integrate feedback.
Step 6. Rest	Spend time with family. Date night. Sleep.
Step 7. Revive	Lead worship with clarity and confidence.
Step 8. Reflect	Meet once a month to assess effectiveness of worship.
Step 9. Retreat	Take one full weekend off every month from preaching.

TABLE 4.2. SAMPLE PREACHING SCHEDULE (SEPTEMBER 2014)

WEEK 1	WEEK 2	WEEK 3	WEEK 4
Wednesday 9/3 9a–4p Write 9/7 sermon.	**Wednesday 9/10** 9a–4p Write 9/14 sermon.	**Wednesday 9/17** 9a–4p Write 9/21 sermon.	**Wednesday 9/24** 6:30p Board meeting.
Thursday 9/4 9a–12p Write 9/7 sermon. 2p–4p Research 9/14 sermon. 6p Rehearse 9/7 sermon with associate(s). Submit final order of service. 7:30p Brainstorm 9/14 sermon with associate.	**Thursday 9/11** 9a–12p Write 9/14 sermon. 2p–4p Research 9/21 sermon. 6p Rehearse 9/14 sermon with associate(s). Submit final order of service. 7:30p Brainstorm 9/21 sermon with associate.	**Thursday 9/18** 9a–12p Write 9/21 sermon. 6p Rehearse 9/21 sermon with associate(s). Submit final order of service.	**Thursday 9/25** 2p–4p Research 10/5 sermon. 6p Worship Arts meeting: review effectiveness of 9/7, 9/14, 9/21 services. 7:30p Brainstorm 10/5 sermon with associate.
Friday 9/5 8a–10a Revise 9/7 sermon. 10a Submit 9/7 sermon for review. 5p Rest. Family. Date night.	**Friday 9/12** 8a–10a Revise 9/14 sermon. 10a Submit 9/14 sermon for review. 5p Rest. Family. Date night.	**Friday 9/19** 8a–10a Revise 9/21 sermon. 10a Submit 9/21 sermon for review. 5p Rest. Family. Date night.	**Friday 9/26** Take one Sunday off a month from preaching to participate in children and youth programs, or take a personal trip with family, or attend professional development events.
Saturday 9/6 8a–10a Integrate feedback from review for 9/7 sermon. Hold Saturday for open office hours and rites of passage. 5p Rest. Family. Date night.	**Saturday 9/13** 8a–10a Integrate feedback from review for 9/14 sermon. Hold Saturday for open office hours and rites of passage. 5p Rest. Family. Date night.	**Saturday 9/20** 8a–10a Integrate feedback from review for 9/21 sermon. Hold Saturday for open office hours and rites of passage. 5p Rest. Family. Date night.	**Saturday 9/27** Off
Sunday 9/7 8a Help prepare worship space. Sound check. Rehearse. 11a Worship.	**Sunday 9/14** 8a Help prepare worship space. Sound check. Rehearse. 11a Worship.	**Sunday 9/21** 8a Help prepare worship space. Sound check. Rehearse. 11a Worship.	**Sunday 9/28** Off

5

Exile Theological and Pastoral Clichés

❖ ❖ ❖ I believe the craft of preaching requires intellectual honesty. God-talk born from banal platitudes diminishes the power of theology. The antidote is for me to master the art of metaphor. I must commit to speaking for myself, promise to do no harm, and transform clichés into gritty, hard-won lessons that claim no celestial rewards. Preaching and pastoral care require intellectual honesty, and let's face it, a great deal of pop theology is dishonest and trite. As a minister, I am required to examine the intent and impact that pop theology has on my congregants' lives, especially when the theology comes in the form of clichés. ❖

Phrases like "It all happens for a reason" are often delivered with an intention of being kind. But the impact of this language can be quite damaging for both the one saying the cliché and those receiving it. For instance, I remember when a woman came to my office in tears. She had told her sisters that her husband was physically abusing her. They gave her financial support and helped her file the divorce papers. Eventually she moved to Philadelphia, found another job, and started a new relationship. In reflecting on the physical abuse she endured—a broken arm and nose, among other things—her brother-in-law said, "Well, maybe everything happens for a reason." She couldn't believe it and neither could

I. In my office she wept, feeling confused and alone: how could someone say that her previous abuse had a reason? She knew that he meant well. It was his way of saying that without the divorce she would not have her new relationship. In this context another cliché comes to mind, "the road to hell is paved with good intentions."

After years of hearing these phrases I decided to publically share my concerns about theological clichés with my congregation. In response, a member asked, "Isn't your critique of the phrase 'everything happens for a reason' insulting to Hindus and Buddhists, specifically as it relates to their belief in Karma?" As I understand it, I explained, Karma places the agency on the individual: the actions that I take now may have consequences later. A more accurate cliché to represent this belief is, "what comes around goes around." I am critical of both viewpoints because the belief in Karma, although it may mean well, can have dangerous effects: generations, civilizations of people have been conditioned to believe that their place in a caste system, their poverty, their illness, or their lack of running water is a direct result of the mistakes they made in their past lives. These harmful beliefs are not only found in Eastern traditions. When I hear the phrase, "what comes around goes around," I can't help but think of the leaders of many Christian religions, including Pope Benedict XVI (Joseph Aloisius Ratzinger), who publicly proclaimed that the AIDS epidemic was God's condemnation for the sin of homosexual behavior. "Everything happens for a reason," right?

These kinds of catchphrases spin in our lexicon as unscrupulous, unexamined theology. I have come to believe that it is a moral imperative for me, in my role as a religious leader, to train my community to use theological language responsibly. This is achieved when we use authentic metaphors to make meaning of our lives rather than to demean one another. Those of us who work in the bowels of human suffering know that God-talk born from banal platitudes diminishes the power of theology and the effectiveness of religion in public life.

For these reasons, I am committed to exile theological and pastoral clichés by applying the following preaching principles to my ministry: I promise to be intellectually honest, to speak for myself, to do no harm, as well as to do good. I share these not to introduce laws that all preachers must follow. Rather, I use this chapter as an opportunity to publicly share the private vows I have made to myself in relationship to the craft of preaching. My hope is that my colleagues will articulate and commit to their own ministerial promises.

1. Be intellectually honest. Be real. Be smart. Do not pretend to know things you do not. Do not be fatalistic, deterministic, or superstitious. Do not adopt a false superiority by using patronizing or condescending language.
2. Speak for yourself. Do not pretend to represent any deity, any prophet, or any sacred text. Speak for yourself and only yourself. Bring integrity and humility to your vocation and be a person of impeccable character.
3. Do no harm. Make meaning. Do not demean others. Put an end to exclusionary, oppressive, and harmful theology.
4. Do good. To "do no harm" is not enough. Do good. Be beneficent. Be kind and generous and use your power to heal, to help, to bless, and to serve.

Those who know me may find it hypocritical of me to express these particular vows, because I, too, have not always been mindful. Many have observed me use my own words to cause harm. Many have seen me tragically fail at these goals for which I am deeply sorry. It is precisely because of my failures that I must regularly and publicly express my intentions.

Such is the work of community. When we enter the sanctuary of community, we ultimately face a vast mirror—at times it may seem like we are looking into circus mirrors; we look thinner than we really are, while other times we look distorted and grotesque. The true mirror of community does not lie, distort, or hide anything. None of us are exempt from truth, not even a minister. Week after week, we come to confront our true selves: to reflect not only on our intentions but to contemplate the impact that our actions have on others. This is the work of a modern religious community: to dig deeper into the nature of our character, to understand our unbridled mistakes, and help one another recover from having broken our vows.

What is the true nature of vows? Are vows a finite product or could it be that vows are inherently a part of a regenerative process? Martin Buber says that we are promise-making, promise-keeping, promise-breaking, promise-renewing people. When we come before the mirror of community we must come as we are, aware that we have broken our vows a thousand times, as Rumi said:

Come, come, whoever you are.
Wanderer, worshipper, lover of leaving, it doesn't matter
Ours is not a caravan of despair.
Come even if you have broken your vow a thousand times,
Come, yet again, come, come.[4]

It is in the context of having failed that I proclaim again the desire to be intellectually honest, to speak for myself, to do no harm, as well as to do good.

In Table 5.1. I have compiled a preliminary list of theological and pastoral clichés. If were to use them I would violate one or more of my vows.

In my estimation, these phrases are filled with ineffective theology that may reflect poorly on me if I were to use them, especially from the pulpit. I do not expect that my ministerial colleagues or members of my religious community will agree with me on all of my selections, nor would I expect them to do so. My hope is that rather than adopt my own list, preachers and congregants will create their own.

What would religion look like if religious communities were to exorcise theological clichés from our collective vocabulary? Take a moment to reflect upon my preliminary list. Scratch out the ones that you do not agree with, put a question mark around the ones you are not sure why are on the list, and circle the ones that you consider to be ineffective. Continue the exercise until you have created the formula for your own exorcism.

I am attracted to preaching that is intellectually honest. I appreciate preachers who are artful about their messages, who create sermons that have elegance without pretense. I admire preachers who are real, smart, and are committed to speaking with integrity and authenticity.

I am troubled when I hear preachers end their sermons about a national tragedy, such as gun violence or a natural disaster, with the mawkish phrase, "Love conquers all." Really? Our neighbor's six-year-old son was shot in the head at school, and the preacher's response is, "Love conquers all"? This is preposterous. How can love conquer all when a tornado just ripped through this home, or when a flood ruined that business? I am determined to simply call it what it is: a tragedy. Tragedies need not be cliché magnets. It is almost as if, when confronted with suffering, people stop thinking. How many times have we heard the phrase, "Everything happens for a reason," or, "What comes around, goes around," or,

"All things work together for good"? These insipid catchphrases are unsophisticated. These comments are not honest, real, or smart. They belittle the experiences of those who suffer while diminishing the effectiveness of those who witness the suffering.

For too long, I have caught myself about to say things such as, "I know how you feel," when I know for certain that I do not. I try to relate to their pain, and I try hard to imagine what it must be like, but I will never know their full experience, nor should I pretend to. My role is not to know what it feels like to have that tragedy happen but to know how the person relates to suffering. My role is to hold people while they weep and to actively listen to them. My role is to be present, and that is often enough. Yet, in these vulnerable moments, I have become unconsciously possessed by clichés. I rarely intend to use them, and still they come: pointless platitudes spill from my mouth. I often do not even know what I mean when I say them.

The same goes for the theological quotas—those predestined, fixed number of celestial rewards—that creep into my speech. After reading *The Secret*, a popular spiritual book about the "law of attraction," I heard myself say when finding a parking spot, "I must be living right." Well, then, I guess because I did something "good," now, with all my powers, I attracted an award. What do I mean when I think that I am alluring good luck? Is luck so weak that it requires me to entice it with my magical thinking? What about the person who was patiently waiting for the space? Did their own negative thinking contribute to me cutting them off and me winning a divine jackpot in the form of a parking spot? What kind of manipulating Deity grants celestial rewards in the form of asphalt? If that is the case, then the woman who lives on the streets, the one I just stepped over to pay my meter, must have done something incredibly bad because she does not even have a car. I suppose she never did enough good to have the chance to play such dippy games. The classist assumptions in these theological quotas leave us to believe it is okay to walk over the body of someone who is literally lying the street. Why? Because we have been doped to believe that there is some divine scorecard.

Theological quotas are fraudulent, whether negative or positive. "I did my good deed for the day," some people say. "Count your blessings," they say. Or my favorite, "No pain, no gain." Does the first one mean that once I do a good deed by 9:53 a.m., I have then met my quota? Do I now have permission to be rude and immoral until sundown? Or does this celestial entity reset the quota clock at midnight, and, if so, in what time zone? Are there really a finite number of blessings that must be counted? Is my pain really necessary for gain? Nonsense. Every dog does not have its day. Every person does not a have finite fifteen minutes of fame. There is no game. There is no test. There is no scoreboard. Theological quotas are rubbish. It is not smart or even wise to pretend that there is some holy tally board used to grant terrestrial or extraterrestrial prizes.

From womb to tomb, we can spend our lives training one another to say absurd things. It is not "always darkest before the dawn." That does not make any sense. Suffering is not a prerequisite for peace. There is no sundown quota that determines the dawn jackpot. The "third time" is not a charm, because I am not enrolled in the Hogwarts School of Witchcraft and Wizardry. There are no charms. It is time I uncross my fingers, stop knocking on wood, and reverently bury the rabbit's foot. I may be Irish, but I do not possess more luck than anyone else. If anything, I need to help Christian societies reflect upon why, exactly, we design buildings without a thirteenth floor. After all, mislabeling high-rises does not erase the fact that there are literally thirteen floors. There is no room for superstitious thinking. There is no time for fatalistic pontifications, as if by "the grace of God" I was saved and everyone else was left to perish.

For the record, I am determined not to, under any circumstances, speak for God. I will not speak for time or for any prophets or for any sacred text. I want to be honest and speak for myself. I do not know if "God has a plan" or if "God helps those who help themselves." I do not have any special powers, and I am not spiritually superior to anyone else. I do not know if "God is willing" or if "God does not give you something you cannot handle." I do not know if the dead "went home to be with the Lord" or if they are "in a better place now." I do not know if "time heals all wounds" or whether "time waits for no one." I do not know if humans have the capacity to "tempt fate" or if there really are "no atheists in foxholes."

If I am to be truly honest, I must recognize that foxholes are likely to be breeding grounds for atheism, because why would God permit or endorse or turn away from war and genocide? Because God is on *our* side, right? Ask any Holocaust survivor about the legitimacy of the theological clichés "God's will" or "tempting fate" or the "law of attraction." Such phrases are insulting and can cause more harm than good. I admire people of humility who choose not to speak for any deity.

The same goes for the Bible. I may draw upon historical evidence about prophets such as Jesus, but given the wide range of scholarly debate about their words and the translations of them, am I in any place to speak for prophets? No. I am, rather, committed to ensure that people know that my interpretations of any passage, biblical or otherwise, can only be attributed to me. By taking the vow not to speak for God, for prophets, or for the Bible, I hope to counter the trend of using biblical justifications to cause harm.

Take, for instance, a murder trial in Colorado in 1995. The jurists sentenced a man to death because of their sole reliance on the biblical passage "an eye for an eye, a tooth for a tooth" (Lev. 24:20–21). They all self-identified as Christians and felt compelled to use their understanding of the Christian Bible as the primary rationale for their decision to authorize capital punishment. The Colorado Supreme Court found the jury's rationale to be unconstitutional and overturned their decision. In addition to misunderstanding the legal parameters of using religious laws to determine civil laws, the jurists also failed to understand the nature of the religious laws outlined in the Christian Bible. In Matthew 5:38–39, Jesus is reported as saying, "You have heard that it was said, 'An eye for an eye and a tooth for a tooth.' But I say to you, do not resist an evildoer. But if anyone strikes you on the right cheek, turn the other also." Hypothetically speaking, let us say the jury was legally permitted to solely rely on biblical laws. Would the outcome have been different if the jury had used Matthew rather than Leviticus? Either way is legally impermissible, the Colorado Supreme court held.

I have found that whether people believe the Bible is nothing more than humanly composed literature or whether they believe it is more than that—the very word of God—it behooves me as a clergyman to teach all the people to examine the affect our beliefs have on others. I can do this by modeling the behavior I wish to see, starting with taking responsibility for how my beliefs inform my own words and deeds. I hope to be a clergyman who teaches citizens to speak for themselves and not scapegoat deities, prophets, or scriptures to justify their own actions. To me, sentencing a person to death because the "Bible told me so" is deeply disturbing. For far too long, religious texts have been used to justify harm. I am committed to the principle that any interpretation of scripture that breeds violence is illegitimate.

I am equally hesitant to counter harmful interpretations of biblical passages with others, such as, "Turn the other cheek," because those too can be dismissed. For instance, Jesus is later reported as saying, "Do not think that I have come to bring peace to the earth; I have not come to bring peace, but a sword" (Matt. 10:34). Given these seemingly contradictory passages, some ask, What would Jesus think about capital punishment? I do not claim to know what Jesus would have thought. I believe that I have a religious duty to people to speak for myself. This begins by exorcising clichés, such as, "The Bible tells me so," from my own thinking.

From the pulpit, I have a dual duty: first, to do no harm, and, second, to do good. It is not enough to resist using harmful speech. I must use my words with intelligence to generate a worthwhile experience in myself and, hopefully, in others. I must be honest and generous and use my power to help somebody, starting with helping myself from not becoming what I set out against. This is what exorcising preaching is all about: to strip myself from notions that cause myself and others harm.

It is not professional or theologically credible for me to use magical thinking to predict unknown calamities or to speak on behalf of celestial entities. My role is to ground my community in the gritty reality that there is suffering. There is and will always be suffering. At times, there are truthful things I can say and do to alleviate pain. These remedies will not come in the form of suspending rational thinking or by reciting enchanted words. These remedies will come in careful deeds—timely and sensitive responses to one another's pain. I do not believe that this pain was willed by some gods, or foreseen by some self-proclaimed prophet, or justified in some sacred text.

I believe that now is the time to model for my congregation how to take shared responsibly for being honest, for speaking for myself, for not only doing no harm but for doing good. The great challenge before us all is to use our power to heal, to help, and to serve one another across the lifespan.

TABLE 5.1. THEOLOGICAL AND PASTORAL CLICHÉS

A blessing in disguise
All things work together for good
Are you saved?
As luck would have it
By the grace of God
Christmas comes but once a year
Count your blessings
Don't tempt fate
Every day is Christmas
Every dog has its day
Everything happens for a reason
Everything happens in threes
Eye for an eye, tooth for a tooth
Fifteen minutes of fame
Fingers crossed
God has a plan
God helps those who help
   themselves
God is in control
God is trying to get your attention
God needed another angel
God willing
God won't give you anything you
   can't handle
God works in mysterious ways
God's green earth
Good deed for the day
Good luck
Guiding light
Heaven's got a plan for you
I know how you feel
I'll pray for you
I must be living right
I'm not into organized religion
I'm spiritual but not religious
If God brings you to it, God will bring
   you through it
In the laps of the gods
It's Adam and Eve, not Adam and
   Steve
It's always darkest before the dawn
Just stay positive
Knock on wood

Law of attraction
Let go and let God
Life is a journey
Lord, have mercy
Love conquers all
Love the sinner, hate the sin
Luck of the draw
Luck of the Irish
Man meant it for evil, but God meant
   it for good
Mills of God grind slowly
Mind over matter
No pain, no gain
No time like the present
S/he went home to be with the Lord
S/he's in a better place now
S/he's with God
The Bible tells me so
The good die young
The Lord will never give you more
   than you can handle
The road to hell is paved with good
   intentions
There are no atheists in foxholes
There are plenty of fish in the sea
There but for the grace of God go I
There is a thin line between love and
   hate
There is one born every minute
Third time's the charm
Time heals all wounds
Time waits for no one
Traditional family values
We create our own reality
What comes around, goes around
When God closes a door, he opens
   a window
When it rains, it pours
Where God guides, God provides
Why do bad things happen to good
   people?
Without benefit of clergy
You'll find someone else

6

Purge Theological Violence

❖ ❖ ❖ I have observed people speak of some religious leaders as a pack of bloodthirsty wolves ravaging the carcasses of secularists. Preachers bolster this impression when they use texts of terror to make theological threats. These have propelled generations of people to leave their religions. This has taught me to vow never to use the pulpit as a weapon, bullying people out of the pews and into theological despair. I can achieve this end by exorcising religious-based bigotry, a practice affirmed in the "Charter for Compassion," which says, "Any interpretation of scripture that breeds violence, hatred or disdain is illegitimate" (www.CharterForCompassion.org). ❖

In 2008, religious scholar Karen Armstrong received a TED Prize—an award presented by the Sapling Foundation under the motto "ideas worth spreading." Armstrong used this global platform to proclaim her wish to spread humanity's greatest idea: the Golden Rule. Her call to action echoed that of the 143 leaders of the Parliament of the World's Religions when proclaiming in 1993 the *Declaration Toward a Global Ethic,* which said, "We must treat others as we wish others to treat us" (www.ParliamentOfReligions. org). In 2009, after collaborating with thousands of people around the world, Armstrong unveiled the "Charter for Compassion" (www.CharterForCompassion.org), designed to inspire people to return the Golden Rule to the center of religious, moral, and political life. In the context of this chapter, the second sentence in the second paragraph and the second point in the third paragraph of the "Charter" serve as antidotes to the pervasive problem of using religion to justify harm. The charter reads as follows:

> *The principle of compassion lies at the heart of all [5] religious, ethical and spiritual traditions, calling us always to treat all others as we wish to be treated ourselves. Compassion impels us to work tirelessly to alleviate the suffering of our fellow creatures, to dethrone ourselves from the centre of our world and put another there, and to honour the inviolable sanctity of every single human being, treating everybody, without exception, with absolute justice, equity and respect.*
>
> *It is also necessary in both public and private life to refrain consistently and empathically from inflicting pain. To act or speak violently out of spite, chauvinism, or self-interest, to impoverish, exploit or deny basic rights to anybody, and to incite hatred by denigrating others—even our enemies—is a denial of our common humanity. We acknowledge that we have failed to live compassionately and that some have even increased the sum of human misery in the name of religion.*
>
> *We therefore call upon all men and women:*
>
> - *to restore compassion to the centre of morality and religion;*
> - *to return to the ancient principle[6] that any interpretation of scripture that breeds violence, hatred or disdain is illegitimate;*
> - *to ensure that youth are given accurate and respectful information about other traditions, religions and cultures;*
> - *to encourage a positive appreciation of cultural and religious diversity;*
> - *to cultivate an informed empathy with the suffering of all human beings—even those regarded as enemies.*
>
> *We urgently need to make compassion a clear, luminous and dynamic force in our polarized world. Rooted in a principled determination to transcend selfishness, compassion can break down political, dogmatic, ideological and religious boundaries. Born of our deep interdependence, compassion is essential to human relationships and to a fulfilled humanity. It is the path to enlightenment, and indispensable to the creation of a just economy and a peaceful global community.*

I draw upon the "Charter of Compassion" to define *texts of terror* as language used by religious communities that "breeds violence, hatred or distain," or language that is used to justify discrimination or oppression. Although these passages may be important in the study of human nature, these texts have sometimes been misconstrued as ordained. As a religious leader, these errors have inspired me to make clear that there is nothing holy about interpreting religious texts to incite violence and to deny people civil and human rights.

World history reveals that leaders, religious and otherwise, have used texts of terror to justify oppression of women, children, homosexuals, animals, and the degradation of the environment. For far too long, these kinds of passages, found in countless religions, have been used to justify invidious discrimination, colonization, slavery, and genocide. This tumultuous history has taught me that I have a moral responsibility to exorcise all forms of theological violence from my ministry and, in turn, from the religious communities I serve. It is urgent for me to refrain from being morally complacent in the face of texts of terror. I believe that there is nothing sacred about religious passages that grant supernatural privileges to savagery.

In *Texts of Terror: Literary-Feminist Readings of Biblical Narratives,* Phyllis Trible examines the tales of violence in which women were victimized, as seen in four portraits: "Hagar, the slave used, abused, and rejected; Tamar, the princess raped and discarded; an unnamed woman [in Judges 19], the concubine raped, murdered, and dismembered; and the daughter of Jephthah [Yifthah], a virgin slain and sacrificed."[7] These are but a few of the problematic portrayals of women in the Bible.

When I attended Union Theological Seminary in New York City, I often found myself becoming emotional when studying these kinds of passages. So much so, that I once stood up to ask my classmates the obvious, "Why is no one else weeping? I don't know what's more troubling, the extreme violence in the Bible or studying with future religious leaders who are desensitized to this horror." My liberal colleagues agreed that the stories were awful but had been raised to gloss over them. Others gave politically correct responses about context and social location. Then they intellectualized their way into the next assignment.

Detach, dismiss, and move on—these were the unwritten recommendations in the invisible curriculum; these, I learned, were survival strategies. Some clergy have used similar tactics. These clergy were taught to remove these passages from the liturgy, to gloss over texts of terror in religious education programs, and to inadvertently mislead generations of people in thinking that the Bible, in its entirety, is poetic, beautiful, and the "word of God." These intellectually dishonest practices result in gross illiteracy.

My role as minister is to help nurture a truly literate people who will know exactly what is in the Bible, to treat texts of terror as evidence of the profound suffering caused by humans, and to refuse to interpret these passages as justifications for breeding violence, hatred, or disdain.

A primary thing I learned in seminary was to exorcise theological violence from my ministry. This was a result of me developing a distinct relationship with texts of terror. I began by refusing to be desensitized or detached. I then gave myself permission to be distressed by the content and to weep over the bloodshed, the hatred, and the fear. I treated my tears as a signal that something was very wrong. Texts of terror became illustrations of human suffering, and I could not, in good conscience, turn away from another's suffering. Rather than dismissing those passages as irrelevant or, worse, interpreting those passages as justifications for the perpetuation of similar acts, I both embraced the torment in the text while refusing to vindicate the violence. This is how reading the Bible became for me a necessary discipline: a way to transform difficult content through the practice of empathetic hermeneutics.

I was disappointed that my seminary did not make this practice a core competency for religious leadership. My disillusionment came not only from the absence of this teaching in the curriculum but also from observing seminarians and professors seemingly treating texts of terror as benign. I was dumfounded by their apparent unconcern for the brutality in the Bible. I kept waiting for them to boldly claim theological authority by vowing to, as religious historian Alfred S. Cole (1893–1977) once said, "Give them, not hell, but hope and courage. Do not push them deeper into their theological despair but preach the kindness and everlasting love of God."[8]

Rather than being riveted by their moral conviction, I observed my colleagues misuse an academic approach to the study of the Bible as a way to detach themselves from the moral responsibility of sensitizing themselves to violence and rejecting any interpretations of texts of terror that may be used to justify harm. Their non-action became my textbook, compelling me to take action in the form of an oath. I used my final exam in systematic theology to vow to never be callous or complacent or nonresponsive to texts of terror. I vowed to be a strong and sensitive moral voice of reason by swearing to publicly repudiate any interpretation of religious texts that was used to justify harm. This was especially true concerning texts of terror that children were taught to be sacred.

❖

According to *The Jewish Children's Bible: Exodus*,[9] there were "15 Good Things God Has Done for Us." Here are two: "God killed the firstborn Egyptians," and, "God gave us the Egyptians' gold and silver." What is good about anyone, or any God, who is theologically justified to kill the children of their enemy? This is deplorable. No child or adult should ever, under any circumstance, be taught that this is "good." It is evil. This evil is multiplied when authors and publishers continue to mislead children to believe that such nauseating messages are sacred. This gross pattern of injustice stems from the book of Exodus, which reads as follows:

> *At midnight the Lord struck down all the firstborn in the land of Egypt, from the firstborn of Pharaoh who sat on his throne to the firstborn of the prisoner who was in the dungeon, and all the firstborn of the livestock... The Israelites had done as Moses told them; they had asked the Egyptians for jewelry of silver and gold, and for clothing, and the Lord had given the people favor in the sight of the Egyptians, so that they let them have what they asked. And so they plundered the Egyptians. (Ex. 12:29, 35–36)*

Whether these passages are shared in the context of a children's class, an adult Bible study group, or a sermon, as a religious leader I have a moral responsibility to consistently issue public refutations against harmful interpretations of texts of terror. Yes, children should be taught about the evils of slavery and how forceful revolts were sometimes necessary; however, under no circumstance should anyone be made to believe that it is "good" for the oppressed to become what they set out against. Children and adults should be consistently told the truth: at one time, people suffered so greatly at the hands of slave owners that the enslaved mistakenly saw their liberation as a theological justification to murder not only their oppressors, but also their offspring. In this bloody context, people should be told what should have happened: rather than killing children as an act of emancipation, the Hebrews should have raised the children of the slave owners to know how to treat all people as they would want to be treated. I consider this to be a responsible treatment of texts of terror—a message that I think should be made explicit in children's Bibles.

I have observed equally disturbing misinterpretations of passages in the Christian New Testament. Take for instance when Jesus is reported making theological threats against the Jewish scribes and Pharisees who "sit on Moses' seat":

Thus you testify against yourselves that you are descendants of those who murdered the prophets. Fill up, then, the measure of your ancestors. You snakes, you brood of vipers! How can you escape being sentenced to hell? Therefore I send you prophets, sages, and scribes, some of whom you will kill and crucify, and some you will flog in your synagogues and pursue from town to town, so that upon you may come all the righteous blood shed on earth, from the blood of righteous Abel to the blood of Zechariah son of Barachiah, whom you murdered between the sanctuary and the altar. Truly I tell you, all this will come upon this generation. (Mt. 23:31–36)

These kinds of passages have been used by some Christians to justify discrimination, oppression, and violence against Jews. Deemed as "sacred," the alleged words of Jesus have been used to persecute Jewish people. For instance, in the gospel of John, Jesus protests the Jews who do not accept his word and condemns them, saying, "You are from your father the devil, and you choose to do your father's desires. He was a murderer from the beginning and does not stand in the truth, because there is no truth in him. When he lies, he speaks according to his own nature, for he is a liar and the father of lies" (Jn. 8:44). The text goes on to say that the Jews "picked up stones to throw at him, but Jesus hid himself and went out of the temple" (Jn. 8:59). The anti-Semitic interpretations of these passages are dangerous and become even more so when used to breed violence, hatred, and disdain.

Take, for instance the passage in Leviticus that says, "If a man lies with a male as with a woman, both of them have committed an abomination; they shall be put to death; their blood is upon them" (Lev. 20:13). These threats are echoed in Romans 1:26b–32 of the New Testament:

Their women exchanged natural intercourse for unnatural, and in the same way also the men, giving up natural intercourse with women, were consumed with passion for one another. Men committed shameless acts with men and received in their own persons the due penalty for their error.

And since they did not see fit to acknowledge God, God gave them up to a debased mind and to things that should not be done. They were filled with every kind of wickedness, evil, covetousness, malice. Full of envy, murder, strife, deceit, craftiness, they are gossips, slanderers, God-haters, insolent, haughty, boastful, inventors of evil, rebellious toward parents, foolish, faithless, heartless, ruthless. They know God's decree, that those who practice such things deserve to die—yet they not only do them but even applaud others who practice them (Rom. 1:26b–32).

As I prepared this manuscript for publication in the spring of 2014, American Christian missionaries and elected officials in Rwanda were literally quoting these passages when introducing bills that made homosexuality a crime, punishable by death. Although leaders in the United States have not been this extreme, Alabama and Texas currently have statutes that require public schools to teach children that "homosexual conduct is a criminal offense." Signers of these bills used these biblical passages to justify criminalizing homosexuality, which, as late as 2003, was deemed unconstitutional by the United States Supreme Court. Ten years later, the high court found unconstitutional the Defense of Marriage Act that restricted the federal definition of civil marriage to one man and one woman. The Court proclaimed that homosexuals deserve equal protection under the law—a civil rejection of religious-based justifications for discrimination. Meanwhile, some religious people and leaders continue to treat biblical passages as vindications of their abhorrent belief that homosexual sex and marriage are unnatural and immoral, and therefore should be outlawed. There are severe consequences to these beliefs.

Generations of people have internalized these texts of terror that mischaracterize homosexuals as less than human. Some have been parents who were theologically justified to disown their gay children. Some were theologically justified to physically attack and murder those perceived to be gay. Some were gay people who internalized the idea that homosexuals "deserve to die" so much that they took their own lives. It is an irrefutable fact that there is a direct correlation between misinterpretations of the theological violence in the Bible and the societal violence against homosexuals. As a minister, I believe it is my role to help society exorcise this evil.

❖

I cannot help but wonder, How long will people continue to donate money to religious groups that promote such hate? How long will conservative seminaries justify these stances and liberal seminaries gloss over them? How long will religious leaders remain complacent about this kind of brutishness? How long will religious people of all kinds claim to be innocent bystanders to texts of terror? I refuse to be that kind of religious person and that type of religious leader.

I vow to exorcise all forms of theological violence from my mind and from my ministry. I promise to be hypersensitive to texts of terror. I promise to never stop being disturbed by the violence in scripture. I aspire to use these texts as teaching tools to demonstrate how these passages and misinterpretations of them can, as the "Charter for Compassion" recognizes, be used to "increase the sum of human misery in the name of religion." I promise to use my power to "work tirelessly to alleviate the suffering of our fellow creatures, to dethrone ourselves from the centre of our world and put another there, and to honour the inviolable sanctity of every single human being, treating everybody, without exception, with absolute justice, equity and respect."

This is what it means to put compassion at the center of my religious life. The Golden Rule is a principle that can help generations and civilizations preserve the inherent worth and dignity of every person, without exception. I have come to believe that the first step in this religious ethic is to refrain from interpreting scripture to intentionally or unintentionally "breed violence, hatred or disdain." To illustrate this point, I close with the words of Sophia Lyon Fahs (1876–1978), who said:

> *Some beliefs are like walled gardens. They encourage exclusiveness, and the feeling of being especially privileged. Other beliefs are expansive and lead the way into wider and deeper sympathies.*
>
> *Some beliefs are like shadows, clouding children's days with fears of unknown calamities. Other beliefs are like sunshine, blessing children with the warmth of happiness.*
>
> *Some beliefs are divisive, separating the saved from the unsaved, friends from enemies. Other beliefs are bonds in a world community, where sincere differences beautify the pattern.*
>
> *Some beliefs are like blinders, shutting off the power to choose one's own direction. Other beliefs are like gateways opening wide vistas for exploration.*
>
> *Some beliefs weaken a person's selfhood. They blight the growth of resourcefulness. Other beliefs nurture self-confidence and ignite the feeling of personal worth.*
>
> *Some beliefs are rigid, like the body of death, impotent in a changing world. Other beliefs are pliable, like the young sapling, ever growing with the upward thrust of life.*[10]

7

Dispel the One-Note Sermon

■ ■ ■ The craft of preaching requires weaving both content and form. The content includes the sermon's theme, subject, and sources. The form is the container used to deliver the content. Not all content can be delivered in the same way. I seek to marry content with form and learn to replace the one-note sermon with a symphony of preaching styles. I have found that this process helps me create a diversity of sermons, keeping the worship services alive week after week. ■

"Begin with the pericope" (pə'rikəpē), the lecturer said in a summer preaching seminar I had attended in Washington, D.C. Seeing the confusion on our faces, he preempted our question by adding, "A pericope is a passage from the Bible." He proceeded to instruct us on how to preach our two assignments. "Begin reading aloud the passages as if we are your congregation—first the passage from the Hebrew Bible, then from the New Testament." He began to write on the board while saying, "Then organize your sermon into the following five parts: (1) introduce what you are planning to say; (2) exegete the text by using scholarly sources to offer a critical interpretation of the passage; (3) present an exposition, a thick description of the biblical lesson; (4) apply the lesson to people's lives; and (5) conclude by summarizing what you said." To me, it sounded like a rendition of the axiom: "Tell them what you are going to say, tell them, then tell them what you told them." This rudimentary five-point formula—similar to what students learn in an expository writing class—posed a dilemma for nearly half of us enrolled in the seminar. We were not from religious traditions with lectionaries, and we came to learn to create contemporary worship. For us, it did not seem appropriate to use this prescription. We bargained with the instructor to use alternate sources and diverse forms. He agreed to allow those of us who did not preach from lectionaries to choose our own source text for one sermon, but he planned to assign us all a specific pericope for our second one. We only preached twice during the twenty sessions, and he expected us all to apply the five-point form to both assignments.

Although we resisted the narrowness of the class, ultimately, we did what we were told. We were obedient students and preached our five-point sermons. Some were good, some were shallow, but most lacked a sense of relevance. It was as if we could have preached those sermons in any WASP suburbia church at any point in the twentieth century. There seemed to be no recognition that the world had recently watched the Twin Towers fall, that the presidential election had felt rigged, and that we had just been thrown into the Iraq War. All this was happening while the adjunct instructor repeated a lesson plan that he seemingly learned during the McCarthy era. There was a severe gap between his knowledge and our context. This may explain why, during class, we buried our heads in our chests while pretending to listen to his daily lectures. I thought it was odd that he spoke more than did all the combined preachers in training. Others agreed, which is one of the reasons he was not invited back to the preaching camp. The main thing his incongruent pedagogy taught me about preaching was what kind of preacher I vowed never to be.

Thankfully, I returned that fall to New York City to the preaching and worship faculty at Union—Janet Walton, Barbara Lundblad, and Troy Messenger. They were exactly the opposite of the lecturer I had just experienced. Their classes were fresh, alive, and inspired. They consistently used emancipatory pedagogy to encourage seminarians to create prophetic, revolutionary worship services. They modeled for us how to integrate multiple artistic mediums and how to experiment with marrying fresh sermon content with a diversity of preaching forms. Their classes were ecumenical laboratories to engage in the moral issues of our time. Thanks to their lessons, I became intellectually and aesthetically engaged in the craft of preaching. These positive experiences were reinforced by the invisible curriculum of New York City, where some of my other teachers of preaching were not ordained.

New Yorkers, with their bold and spirited ways, exposed me to unconventional brands of worship.

Worship, in one form, means to *scribe worth,* to *etch meaning.* I met New Yorkers who used their suffering to scribe into the cityscape reflections of our shattered humanity while etching visions of a world made whole. They were the underground singers, dismissed and deranged, pelting the swarms of subway commuters with their songs. They were the playwrights, whose prophecies in the form of monologues were heard only between the squeaks of the off- off-Broadway playhouse seats.

Yet, the poets, with their sidewalk chalk and their soapboxes, were the ones who captured the rhythmic convictions of the tired and tempest-tossed. In times past, poets would have been presented with laurel wreaths and the title "Oracle," but now they were busboys in Times Square and cocktail waitresses in East Side cigar bars. The slam poets at the Nuyorican Café were, to me, the East Village archbishops—guardians of noncanonical wisdom.

When slam poets preached, people gathered. These were the poets with whom we came to worship—to scribe meaning, to etch for ourselves some sense, some self-worth. I did not care how long I needed to be in the sedated processional, down the dark, rank wind tunnels of Alphabet City, because the *Autobiography of Malcolm X* had lit my mind. Malcolm's life became my sacred text as I pilgrimaged on the one train back and forth to Harlem. Once downtown, I did not care how thick the huddled masses crawled up the sanctuary walls of the Nuyorican. The East Village became, at least for that night, our promised land.

Poet after poet slammed one image into the next. Exorcising the sentimental with their gritty wit, they struck fire to pretense and found elegance in adversity. They were more than masters of the spoken word; they were ethicists and artists and watchdogs and mourners and patriots and anarchists who praised daybreak despite the rancid city sunrise. In return for the poets' sacrifice, the gathered tribe made offerings through foot stomping and hand whacking and throat wailing. We, the worshipers, deserted our barstool pews for the streets.

I left awed by the simplicity of the form. People gathered. Poets spoke. There was ritual in the spoken word. There was ritual to the unspoken longing to no longer be isolated beings in a sea of urban anonymity. Such was the power and the glory of that untamed sanctuary.

❖

That summer in D.C., Malcolm's story continued to quake in my muscles as I crawled through the humidity to the preaching seminar. I sheepishly entered the barren chamber possessed by the lecturing man of the cloth. Attending class was drudgery. Preparing a five-point sermon was a bore. The week earlier, I scrapped three drafts of my doltish "exegete" of the assigned "pericope." I thought the lecturer's lingo was as anachronistic as was the required text—the parable that equated heaven to leavened yeast (Mt. 13:33). I could not bear to speak about such clichéd irrelevance.

I finally broke the mold and submitted the assignment in the spirit of Nuyorican rebellion. I débuted a distinct form: the slam sermon. Malcolm X's life was my source text, and slam poetry was my vessel. I treated this moment as the first of many exorcisms in absolving the one-note sermon from my ministry.

Listed here is an excerpt. The full text and a multimedia presentation can be viewed at www.ExorcisingPreaching.com.

Muscle Memory: A Slam Sermon

(the pericope)

a reading from the autobiography
of malcolm x, chapter
life, verse rape:

"you see me—... in the streets
they used to call me detroit red. yes!
yes, that raping, red-
headed devil was my grandfather!
that close, yes!
my mother's father!..."

"if i could drain away
his blood that pollutes
my body, and pollutes
my complexion.
i'd do it! [i'd do it!]..."

"because i hate every drop of the
rapist's blood that's in me! the
rapist's blood that's in me! [the
rapist's blood—] and it's not just me,
it's all of us!"[11]

(introduction)

blessed be—it's all of us—
may we hear this word—it's all of us—
in our muscle pulsing
on our breath, pulsing

we open the gospel
of the non-canonical
prophetic voices quaking underground
trains of thought dancing in our
breath, railroading on our corpse
don't give me that—

that innocent blank face, saying
you can't remember
"having not yet discerned"
saying you can't remember
what you never learned

it's time we break
the ignorance of our blood
it's for your sake
we must look at every drop
asking, would you

drain away
the history that pollutes
your pretty story
tainting your body,
your complexion
ever rotting
your muscle memory

with time, we exegete
carving the pulse
with time, we defeat
what we thought
had never been, it's time i
slam this sermon

(exegesis)

malcolm.
born omaha.
home burned in lansing.

father murdered.
mother deemed insane.
a diploma of dope in roxbury.
harlem his college.
master's?—penitentiary.

and yet, an ivy guest at harvard,
columbia, brown, and penn
malcolm little not interested
in being american,
cuz the good ole' u.s. of a. still
ain't interested in him

I continued to use the five-point rubric to slam my sermon. Although the lecturer did not select it as one of the sermons to be preached during the seminar, I did receive a passing grade and two graduate credits. The most rewarding outcome of the experience was delivering myself from the idea that all sermon content must fit into a single form. I knew this was false, as did the permanent preaching faculty at Union. My hope is that the ideas scribed here will be received as an invitation for new and seasoned preachers to experiment with not only what they preach on but also how they preach it.

I dedicate the rest of this chapter to highlighting some of the forms I have used over the years.

Source Text: Direct Experience

In my tradition, direct experience is as legitimate a source as is any sacred text. (See Appendix A, the first source in "Principles and Sources of Unitarian Universalism"). Direct experiences point to a kind of *a priori* knowledge, a wisdom that begins from a latent frame of understanding and is tested and confirmed by our observations. By sharing one another's experiences, members of the community treat with reverence and respect one another's unique point of view. Unlike creedal-centered religions, Unitarian Universalism does not mandate uniformity in belief or practice. The goal is to understand one another, and understanding does not imply agreement. This courteous treatment of one another's direct experiences can create a nondefensive culture for searching, for learning, and for finding one's voice.

At the First Unitarian Church of Philadelphia, I was pleased to observe many people engage in various communication techniques. One leader had spent time at a Zen Buddhist retreat learning about a mindfulness training titled "deep listening and loving speech." Two other leaders had recently returned from a conference on nonviolent communication; others had returned from trainings on appreciative inquiry. Their experience with these models became of great value to the community. Together, the leaders summarized these practices in the church's Communications Toolkit (downloadable at www. ExorcisingPreaching.com).

The toolkit became my source text for a sermon titled "Language as a Generative Act." I drew upon the direct experience of the coauthors of the toolkit, along with the experience of several members of the church who were perplexed by my preaching style. Several long-time members were confused by the diversity of my services. They had been accustomed to the preacher standing in the same place, wearing the same robe, and offering similarly styled sermons week after week. I decided to use their concerns as an opportunity to poke fun at myself.

Form: Conversation

After choosing the toolkit as my source text, I determined a conversational form. In this context, it would have not been appropriate for me to stand behind a historic pulpit, towering above the congregation to preach from a booming microphone. I had to be on the ground, at the congregants' level. There could not be anything between us, even a script. I had to simply speak the sermon as if it were a conversation between friends. The conversational form was anything but spontaneous. I memorized an outline of the sermon and rehearsed the ideas with my worship associates. It ultimately came across as if it was extemporaneous.

In contrast to the conversational tone, I decided to wear a robe, which was rare for me. I did so because it became another tool to use humor to transform the insulting, homophobic comments that people said about my garb.

Below is a transcript of the first four minutes of my sermon. Notice that my grammar is bad and my syntax is clunky. That is the price and beauty of choosing a less formal form. A video recording can be found at www.ExorcisingPreaching.com.

I've heard lots of different critiques of our ministry together. And sometimes people can be very unmindful with their speech.

They might say, for instance, "Oh, that minister. That minister is too theatrical. I can't believe it. It's just too much. We are applauding in the church. Everything is such a production. He has his own YouTube channel. He even has his own dot-org. Do you realize that he is so narcissistic that he even dresses like Liberace?"—for example.

In those times, someone hearing that information might say, "You know I've been hearing about direct communication. It's a practice in our toolkit. And I'm wondering if you feel comfortable going to Nate to express your concerns. Oh, you do? Okay. Let me know how it goes. Oh, oh, you don't? Okay, would you like me to go with you?" And something happens. That road, that very attractive road of gossip, of unmindful speech, of using words to harm, might lure somebody. But if held in community, that person may be able to transform their language and help be more constructive in their speech. Or they might just take all the things they just said and put it into an e-mail and cc 83 of their personal friends—for instance.

I share these little things because there is something magical that happens here each and every week. We ground ourselves in the power of living intentionally. We ground ourselves in the power of living in community, which is messy. All kinds of complicated things can happen, and we may get very upset or emotional about certain changes. For example, you might see a change like the chalice, which is normally on this pedestal—was actually moved over here. "And do you know that I have been on the Chalice Committee for 83 years, and we have never moved that chalice there. I am so angry that I want to throw the piano bench at you."

Now, if someone said that to you before you looked at the toolkit, you may have interpreted that as a threat. But now that you are so spiritually mature and you learned all these great techniques, you might actually consume the information differently. You might think, "Wow, my friend is really upset." I wonder if my friend who is speaking to me in that way about this chalice, I wonder if that's how they speak to their partner, or their children, or themselves. And in this way, we use our imagination to put ourselves in the other person's shoes, and we start to apply the techniques of nonviolent communication and help them express their needs. "Oh, it sounds like you have a need to be respected. I am sorry. We are all roommates in this great, beautiful home, and I didn't consult you about that matter, and I wasn't being a very good roommate. I'm sorry. But to clarify, it is not appropriate for you to throw the piano bench at somebody, right? You know that? Good." We can both set boundaries and use our language to open up meaning rather than to demean one another.

I proceeded to "exegete" additional practices from the Communication Toolkit. My conversational form drew upon the direct experiences of members in our community. Their lives, their words were my primary texts. I wonder how stilted it would have sounded had I attempted to jam this content into a five-point sermon and preach it from behind a pulpit on high. Would I have missed an opportunity to minister had I been bound to preach about a predetermined lectionary text? The art of exorcising preaching is found in freeing oneself and one's community from ruts and routines.

I have seen a number of unintended consequences when religious communities train people to expect the same thing week after week. Religious leaders make this choice because they want to bring comfort to people's ever-changing lives by offering something stable and predictable. I respect this view; however, it can result in training people to be rigid, closed, and irritated by change. For this reason, I have spent years questioning religions that use lovely, intentional means to unintentionally breed harmful ends.

Do not religious leaders have a moral responsibility to train people to embrace ambiguity with maturity? Is it not our duty to nurture the ethics of flexibility and openness and curiosity and kindness? This does not mean we need to abandon all ritual or strip away all that is familiar. Rather, what if a diversity of expressions becomes the norm? What if a plurality of voices and ideas and beliefs becomes the contemporary cannon, co-written by all members of a living tradition? What if all the different sources and forms become symbols of a larger mission and vision to help one another build a beloved community?

In this next excerpt, I try to capture the spirit of this philosophy while also offering bold definitions of our religious community and of my role as minister. A video clip can be found at www. ExorcisingPreaching.com.

We no longer want to be isolated beings in a sea of urban anonymity. We want to feel a part of a deeply woven, interconnected web of life and bound by the moral fabric that nurtures our shared destiny. We want to be co-creators in the pursuit of building that beloved community—where no person, no person, is alien to our compassion, where the young and the old are renewed in one another's company.

And this is why we gather week after week. Our liturgical calendar is based not on the rotation of ancient scriptural passages but on the social gospel of the modern timetable of urgency. We gather to shine light on the shadows of our days. We gather to be relevant, to be on the pulse of humanity's suffering, and to respond to the moral issues of our time with care. In this way, we come to church not to save our souls but to save ourselves from the religious bigotry that uses faith to harm and not heal. Coming to community moves us beyond the preoccupations of our own pains: to reach up and out and into the eyes of our neighbor across the arc of the world; to look up and out and into the teary eyes of our neighbor sleeping on the curb across the street. We spend our time using our faith not to condemn those who believe differently but to use compassion and equity and justice as tools by which to tend to all our relations. When doing so, we build that beloved community.

So if anyone asks, "Why have we welcomed two hundred new members to our church and why have two thousand people been coming in and out of our community center week after week? Why have 23,000 people listened to our podcasts? Why is this congregation engaged in community organizing?" the answer is that it's because we ain't no social club. We ain't no intellectual secret society, and we ain't no navel-gazing hum-diddy-dum cult. We are an intentionally diverse congregation. We are a group of people who want to lead meaningful lives, to love one another without prejudice, and to build a just and sustainable world.

So when you come to me, come not with the expectation to have some passive clergyman coddle you into complacency. No. Come to me as your PST, your personal spiritual trainer. I'm serious. I want to see you move. I mean it. I want to see you root yourself in community based on moral complexity and to hold one another to the ethic of intellectual honesty. I want to see you move beyond the religious hang-ups of your broken past and use your regenerative spirit to seize the day. I want to see you flex your moral muscles. I want to see you exercise spiritual practices to the point of training your mind and body and spirit to collaborate as a single, integrated, and dynamic entity. I want to hear you articulate your beliefs. I want to hear you articulate your faith to the point of having some moral relevance. I want to know that you are engaged in the issues of our time. I want to know what makes you afraid. I want to know if you are cultivating your doubts and your questions so that when you do take a stand, we can all trust your authenticity. I want to know the intricacies of how you are treating other people. Have you learned new ways to better your relationships? If so, share them. I want to know if you have learned to like yourself. Have you learned to love yourself? I want to know if you feel alive. I want to know if you feel like you belong, like you feel like you matter, because to me, you do. You do.

Just look around. You are amazing people. You are surrounded right now by a sea of amazing, beautiful, courageous people who are building that beloved community and standing on the side of love. Aware that building community is not easy, we close with the words of Martin Luther King Jr., who is said to have been in this sanctuary when he first learned of nonviolent civil disobedience. He said, "When I speak of love, I am not speaking of some sentimental and weak response. I am speaking of that supreme, unifying principle of life. Love is somehow that key that unlocks the door," King said.

So whether you are joining our collective effort to restore the self-worth of our neighbors by promoting literacy or whether you are serving our Haitian brothers and sisters by preserving their dignity, know that you, you have the keys to the city of love—keys that call us to unlock the doorway of light so as to transform a shadow land of suffering into a truly beloved community.

Personal Spiritual Trainers

In this sermon, I defined the congregation as a moral training ground and its minister as a personal spiritual trainer. I went on to explain that ministers are not the only ones who play the role of a PST. It is a shared responsibility. We all take up the charge to teach one another how to lead meaningful lives, to love one another without prejudice, and to build a just and sustainable world.

I explained that the congregation is a type of roundhouse, similar to the turning houses in railroad yards. Trains from different directions come into the massive gazebo-like structure. The trains are unloaded, repaired, retooled, and turned around. The trains are sent off into various directions. Such is the role of the congregation: to foster a culture in which a diversity of people can help one another unload our burdens, to seek healing, and to equip ourselves with new tools. Week after week, we turn one another around, resulting in our personal and collective transformation. We are sent out into the unknown where there are not always clear tracks to our destination, but there is always a way home.

There have been several key moments in my ministry in Philadelphia when my personal spiritual trainers witnessed my moral failures and then gently, yet firmly, called me back to my better self. They reminded me of my own aspirations and helped turn me toward a day worth living. Take for instance the following words that I shared with the congregation:

We, as one strong body, are required to lead by being. When we feel the impulse to be the interrogator, we must choose to be the generator of visions larger than ourselves. When we feel the impulse to be enraged, we must accept the invitation to be empathetic and no longer make people the object of our aggression. When we feel the impulse to be furious, let us dare to be curious. When we feel the impulse to be righteous, let us transform our soapbox into a music box. Let us dare to be powerfully playful.

I explained that we needed to lead by being kind and generous. We could not seek peaceful ends through hostile means. We could not attend the upcoming peace rally if we were addicted to rage. We could not, in the name of peace, mangle our faces with anger, ratchet our shoulders with contempt, and righteously scream into the ether.

I took an ontological approach to reflect upon the *nature of being* in the context of doing justice work. I was a philosopher that day, a theorist casting an untested hypothesis about the ontology of being. These were lovely words to share on a Sunday morning. The problem was that Tuesday rolled around.

The Occupy Wall Street rally was in full force. I was in lower Manhattan interviewing the peaceful protestors and taking photos. Then I headed to New York University to meet my partner for a lecture he was dying to see. As we arrived in the lecture hall and took our seats, I received a notification on my phone from the Associated Press: Mayor Bloomberg instructed the police to remove the occupiers. I was upset that citizens were denied their constitutional right to peacefully assemble and petition their grievances.

Just before the start of the lecture, my partner went to the restroom. A woman in pearls took his seat, and her husband threw my partner's coat on the ground. I was enraged. When I told them that the seat was taken, the woman in pearls said, "We sponsored this event."

That was it. From zero to sixty miles per hour, I said, "Oh, you're the 1 percent. I've been meaning to meet you." I asked her, "Do you own the chair or the whole theater?" In reaction to her nonresponse, I said, "You must be someone really important. Are you famous? If not, let me help you be." I took out my phone and started taking her photo.

I confess the full story in the sermon "Are You the 1 Percent?" (Appendix C). The sermon was about my moral failures. The form was a confession. I admitted to the congregation that in the pursuit of theater-seat justice, I was an ass. I not only sought to humiliate her, but I also humiliated myself. I was a hypocrite, unable to take my advice about being kind in the midst of adversity. In that context, I featured the words of a member of the congregation, Ranwa Hammamy, who had just been admitted to Union Theological Seminary.

I showed Ranwa the picture and while giggling, I said, "Look at [the woman in pearls]. Look at her face. And look at those behind her, gasping with fear." Ranwa paused then asked me a powerful, spiritually mature question: "Nate, why are you keeping the picture?" My chin fell to my chest. I answered her honestly: "Maybe it's pride. I feel wronged, and I want to gloat." Her question gave me the opportunity to reflect. I have come to realize that inside of me is a deep-rooted scorecard that rewards me for humiliating people. It cries out like a master of ceremonies at a Tuesday Circus, "Step on up, boy; you just got a point for *being* witty. Yes. There you go; here's another for *being* sarcastic. Ding, ding, ding. You showed her." By many standards, my do-justice card was chock full with points. But here's the thing. That's not my scorecard. My true scorecard is up there, on the pulpit with that Sunday reading. It's the scorecard that is kept each time Unitarian Universalists gather to remember why we do justice work in the first place. I have to be honest. It's really hard for me to earn those kinds of Sunday points when living a Tuesday kind of life. I'm down here one day and up there another day. I'm in the struggle. I'm in that struggle for an integrated life, where my public words match my private deeds—where my private thoughts mirror my deepest ideals.

In this confessional sermon, the pulpit became the focus point. The pulpit became a symbol of the place where we express our most nourishing desires. As you can see in the video (www. ExorcisingPreaching.com), I walked up and down the stairs of the chancel, metaphorically illustrating the chasm that lay between my aspirations and my actions. I confessed to needing the community to hold me accountable for my Sunday ideals. I asked it to hold me in care when, on Tuesday, I fail to make those values a reality. I publicly thanked Ranwa for being my personal spiritual trainer, and, during the sermon, I deleted the photo from my phone. The congregation applauded.

The Wisdom of Congregants, the Humanity of Clergy

I have learned to treat the wise words and generous deeds of members of the congregation as sacred text. I have been committed to use my sermons as platforms to reward the congregants' outstanding behavior, modeling for us all how to treat the community as a moral training ground. We all share in the responsibility in being one another's personal spiritual trainers.

One year, I posted on Facebook an invitation for people to submit sermon topics. (See chapter 3, "Democratize the Pulpit.") A man I will call Jorge had been following our online ministry from Florida. He asked, "How do I love someone seemingly unlovable?" I had a series of pastoral e-mail exchanges with Jorge, in which he revealed the context of his question. As a child growing up in Chicago, he had been sexually abused. He wanted to know how he could forgive.

I sent him a copy of a book called *Before Forgiving: Cautionary Views of Forgiveness in Psychotherapy,* edited by Sharon Lamb and Jeffrie Murphy. Contributors warned those in the helping professions to resist the urge to idealize theologies of forgiveness. Generations of battered women were told by their clergy to return home and forgive their abusive husbands. I told Jorge that this proved to be a form of theological violence: a general belief that when applied in that particular context can put victims in harm's way.

I asked him to think about putting more emphasis on the truth and reconciliation that comes before forgiving. A colleague of mine in Florida was particularly gifted with this kind of work. I connected Jorge with her, and she provided him pastoral support. He ultimately became a member of her congregation. In thanks, Jorge sent me a note lamenting that he had never seen, in person, the Tiffany stained-glass windows in our historic sanctuary. I sent him a photo of the angel featured above the chancel. Her colorful wings span across the glass, and she stands on a band of stars, surrounded by joyous faces of angelic children. When caught by sunlight, the angel has light skin; and, during the night, she has dark skin. She has become an important symbol of our multicultural congregation. One Sunday I reflected upon the question, how do you love someone seemingly unlovable, the multicolored angels became our focus point.

Connie Simon, another one of my personal spiritual trainers, started the service by saying, "Nate asked me a question a couple of days ago. He said, 'How do you love someone seemingly unlovable?' I looked him dead in the eye and said, 'You just do.' He was surprised by my answer. You should have seen the look on his face. It was priceless." Connie went on to share her direct experience. (An audio recording is hosted at www.ExorcisingPreaching.com.)

We UUs believe in love as a universal principle. But what does that really mean? Would I go out of my way to love someone who hurt me? Do I have to forgive everyone who hurts me? I asked myself, "Could I love Louis"—the drunk driver who killed my big brother in 1998?

I strive to emit a positive, healthy energy at all times. When I look through my mind's eye, I see the world as filled with these multicolored particles of energy. Those who emit this energy are putting it out there to share. Those who are able will receive it and use it and pass it on. This to me is a kind of love. Sure, there are deeper kinds of love that move me to go out of my way to help you, to be kind to you, to do things for you, and to love you physically. But with regard to this first universal kind of love—the emission of my energy, yes, I do love everyone.

And Louis, he puts out something that is a different color. And my body rejects that. I don't stop my energy from going his way, but because of who he is, he cannot attract the most loving particles, and that's OK. I'll be honest; if I saw him about to be hit by a train, I'm not always sure I would rush to his aid.

The day after my brother Doug was killed, I wouldn't have lifted a finger to stop that train. Today, I don't know. I stood in a courtroom about a year ago and testified at *another* one of Louis's hearings after he had been picked up for DUI number thirty-something. I didn't do it for personal satisfaction or for vengeance but to keep Louis off the streets so he cannot hurt anyone else. So, yes, when I stood in that courtroom and told the judge that Louis should go back to jail, I was loving Louis and loving myself even more. I don't let him hurt me anymore.

I won't send out hate and let him affect the color of what I am putting out into the world. I want to emit *all* the pretty colors. And so this morning, I come to this beautiful place to partake of your beautiful loving energy and to share mine with you. And to do that, we start the same way we do every Sunday by saying, simply, "Welcome home."

The congregation joined Connie in unison to say, "Welcome home," a hallmark of our worship. She served as the spiritually mature trainer, modeling how to be both strong and caring. Without knowing Jorge or the context of his question, she showed how it is possible to confront one's perpetrator and lovingly set boundaries. But maybe Jorge needed to hear another response, one less skillful. That was my job: to illustrate for him and for others how hard it is to love someone who has harmed you.

Rather than walk up the stairs to the historic pulpit, I sat in the first pew. I listened to our music director sing Leonard Cohen's "Hallelujah." Then we sat in silence to meditate on Cohen's words: "There is a crack, a crack in everything / That's how the light gets in."

Out of the silence, I stood at the pew. I looked up at the angel and began to speak to her. For the first time in my career, I prayed a sermon. Loving the unlovable was the subject and prayer became the form. I said to the multicolored angel, "I know we have never spoken before, but I see you: your colors, your strength, your beauty, surrounded by the innocent who are casting wishes from beyond…" I proceeded to offer a confessional prayer to the stained glass—the window being a symbol of our highest aspirations. I said:

How do I love someone seemingly unlovable? I have to confess that my answer is simply, you don't. You don't. When I hear Connie speak of the time when her brother was killed by a drunk driver, and I think, if she were to come here in this space, to fall and weep into my arms and cry out that her brother is now dead because of the irresponsible acts of another, am I honestly supposed to say, "Love Louis. Love the guy who killed your brother"? Am I honestly supposed to say, "Forgive him"? Am I honestly supposed to do what different religions have been doing throughout time and put the burden on the victim? I can't.

My prayer was a reflection of what people have told me in pastoral sessions. My prayer was an expression of my struggle for an intellectually honest and gritty religious response to tragedy. As a ministerial authority, it was essential for me to authentically express doubt. Balanced by Connie's wisdom, born from her direct experience, those gathered would receive permission to struggle while at the same time be inspired by one among them transcending that struggle.

Together, Connie and I created an aesthetically compelling and morally challenging experience. She played the role of the spiritually grounded, ethically superior congregant, which allowed me to play the role of the doubtful, vulnerable clergyman—a role that made clear that their pastor would not theologically coerce them in times of struggle. This mission was driven by the vision of a church as a training ground, where we worked out our deepest concerns—a sanctuary that was strong enough to contain our most acute traumas.

❖

A Letter to My Murderer

On Sunday, July 27, 2008, Jim David Adkisson walked into the sanctuary of the Tennessee Valley Unitarian Universalist Church as twenty-five children and youth performed the musical *Annie*. Adkisson opened a guitar case, pulled out a 12-gauge shotgun, and began firing. Two Unitarian Universalists were killed: Greg McKendry and Linda Kraeger. Seven more were injured. Three congregation members and one visitor restrained Adkisson before the police department responded to the 911 call.

Adkisson's ex-wife had been a member of the Tennessee Valley Church in the 1990s but was no longer a member. Adkisson's hatred of liberalism, including his hatred for the church's acceptance of homosexuality, was expressed in a letter found by police. In an affidavit, one of the police officers who interviewed Adkisson said, "he had targeted members of the church because of its liberal teachings and his belief that all liberals should be killed because they were ruining the country… [H]e felt that the Democrats had tied his country's hands in the War on Terror and…had ruined every institution in America with the aid of major media outlets." Adkisson stated that because he could not get to the leaders of the liberal movement that he would then target those who had voted them into office." Adkisson had also stated that he intended to keep firing until the police killed him. It did not get to that point, because members of the congregation tackled him and held him until the police arrived. He was given the right to legal representation and a fair trial, at which time he pleaded guilty to two counts of murder and accepted a life sentence without parole.

Unitarian Universalists around the globe were traumatized. In response, I sent out a pastoral letter via video (www. ExorcisingPreaching.com). While filming, my cat jumped on my lap and faced the camera. Together, my feline cohost and I invited people to come to a special worship service that Sunday. Hundreds and hundreds of congregations did the same. As a united denomination, we stood in solidarity with all those in Knoxville who were simultaneously consecrating their sanctuary as a safe and holy place.

During the fall, I joined with members of the church to reflect upon Adkisson's sentencing. The state of Tennessee has had the death penalty since the 1800s. From 2000 to 2007, four men convicted of murder had been killed by the state: three by lethal injection and one by electrocution. Would Unitarian Universalists in Tennessee, and throughout the denomination, advocate for Adkisson's lethal injection? We informally polled our Philadelphia congregation and found that around 13 percent favored capital punishment for Adkisson.

Aware that our church was both a training ground for the moral issues of our time and a container for our suffering, I dedicated a service to the subject of capital punishment. I had long wondered whether an "advanced directive" could serve as a powerful legal analogy for overturning the death penalty. We are granted the legal right to determine our end-of-life care, writing in our wills our desire to have no heroic medical interventions, otherwise known as D.N.R. (do not resuscitate) or A.N.D. (allow natural death). If I could legally set the moral parameters for my death, could I do the same if I were murdered? Could I draft an advanced directive, of sorts, that would inform the state of my end-of-life wishes if someone were to take my life? I titled the sermon "A Letter to My Murderer" (Appendix D).

In the service I read aloud my "letter," beginning: "June 27, 2009. Dear Mr. Adkisson: If you are reading this letter, you have taken my life. I am dead. You are alive. I write this letter without knowing your motives for killing me. I also do not know the events in your own life that contributed to your actions. I do know, however, that my family must be in excruciating pain." I proceeded to express my anger, saying, "No one who takes a life deserves to continue living."

As a rhetorical tool, I used theologically violent language. To my congregation's surprise, I said, "We must do God's work by sentencing you to death." The people froze in their pews as I said, "My dying wish is that whatever pain you may have caused me, you yourself may experience. My dying wish is that my family members can, if they desire, be present for your execution." I continued to emotionally escalate the letter to the point that two members of the congregation forcefully walked out of the service.

I began to get emotional while reading the rest of the letter. My speech was broken, and I paused in contemplation: "I wonder if you ever knew love. I wonder if there will be...I wonder... Will this letter...the one composed to you now...will it ever have my signature?" I then said, "God, give me the strength to sign this letter... God, give me the strength...give me the strength to write another." Then I crumpled the letter. The worshipers collectively exhaled. The content was designed to aesthetically reflect the religious and political beliefs of some of those who believe in capital punishment. I used the sermon as a mirror to reflect back some of the voices on this debate.

I then pulled out a second letter: "June 27, 2009. Dear Mr. Adkisson: If you are reading this letter, you have taken my life. I am dead. You are alive. You have received a fair trial and were found guilty. The state will inevitably choose an appropriate punishment for you; it is not my role to affirm or deny the court's decision. My faith lies in the system. I know that those in power will do what is right." In this second letter, I relinquished my rights to the state, a dramatic symbol of many people's attitudes. This second letter reflected a kind of powerlessness, concluding with the belief of many, "It is not as if anything I say here will matter anyway."

I crumpled that letter, too, and began reading a third: "June 27, 2009. Dear Mr. Adkisson: If you are reading this letter, you have taken my life. I am dead. You are alive. I may be dead, but my life continues through the memories of my loved ones. My life continues through the legacy of these words. I am aware of my power. I am aware of my responsibility. I am aware that my words may help determine your fate."

I dedicated the rest of the letter to represent the beliefs of those who are trying to overthrow capital punishment laws. I said, "I believe that allowing you to live will be the most just punishment. Death is easy. Life? Life is hard. My dying wish is that you live. You must learn to live with yourself; you must live with the past; you must live with your sentence."

I proceeded to express my desire for him to be removed from society, to serve time, and to be sentenced to tending to a garden. I wanted him to nurture life. When he was deemed ready, I wanted him to be given the responsibility to care for a cat named Nate. "I want you to take care of your new animal companion. Treat him with dignity, just as you seek to preserve your own. Discipline him with care, just as you discipline yourself by practicing self-care." I added, "Therein lies your charge: to use your power to preserve my memory, to use your power to preserve your dignity, to use your power to preserve life."

"I close my letter with some questions for you. What will you do with your new life? What purpose will come from these events? What vision will you craft for yourself? Just as these questions are asked of you, one question remains for me: Will this letter receive my signature?"

I then stepped away from the lectern and said to the congregation, "Just as I ask this of myself, another question remains: it is not, Which of these three letters will receive my signature; the question is, Which of these letters will you write?"

The form of a letter can be a powerful vehicle for engaging people's moral imagination. I would not have been able to have the same emotional impact had I drafted a five-point sermon. I needed a container that could hold this complex message. I was not only talking about a murderer who targeted Unitarian Universalists. I was talking about the complications of capital punishment, at the same time introducing the idea of an "LPad," a Life Penalty Advanced Directive (as further explored in the "Agenda Setters" video featured at at www.ExorcisingPreaching.com).

Given the complexity of these intersecting subjects, the form had to be remarkably simple. A personal letter, crumpled up and rewritten twice over, helped me to layer the themes in an emotionally accessible way. I could have written an academically detached, soapbox sermon filled with legalese, but would I have been persuasive? Maybe. Would I have created a space where people's minds and hearts were open? Not necessarily. Would I have been able to model how to train my mind, body, and spirit to collaborate as a single, integrated, and dynamic entity? Doubtful.

At the monthly worship arts meeting, I was told that for many, this three-letter method was challenging, complex, and captivating. The offended couple that left during the first sermon I knew had a different experience, which is why I called them that Sunday afternoon. They did not pick up. Apparently, they were busy furiously writing a letter justifying their refusal to pledge money to the church. In my voice message, I brought their attention to an e-mail I had just sent them that attached all *three* of the letters. For them, *three* was the magic word. They called me that night to invite me to meet them at their home.

When I arrived, to my surprise, they gave me a group hug. They were so incredibly relieved to hear that I was using the three letters as rhetorical tools to make a larger point. We spent the evening talking at length about the purpose and potential of the LPad idea, which they liked a great deal—so much so that over the next year they helped book for me a half-dozen speaking engagements, including at the national General Assembly of Unitarian Universalist congregations. Members from around the country joined us, including from Tennessee. These events inspired a dozen people later to write me, confirming that they had added their own LPads to their wills. I was so pleased to see that the letters had an impact beyond the walls of our sanctuary.

❖

A Letter to Monsanto

The summer of the Knoxville shootings was also the time when delegates at the General Assembly voted to study the issue of ethical eating. Communities throughout the country agreed to examine the moral complexity of food—its production, consumption, and environmental impact. I did so by facilitating an adult religious education class. We met weekly for eight weeks. It was such an invigorating experience that members of the class asked me to take what we had learned to the pulpit. The problem was that the intersecting issues related to the ethics of food were so massive that I could have preached for days, as if it were some political filibuster. Instead, I chose to focus only on the controversial subject of genetically modified foods—a huge subject itself.

I began to classify my questions into themes, and I spent days vigorously collecting research, which made it that much more difficult to concisely communicate the kernel of each issue. There was too much to explore in too little time. The early drafts of the sermon felt foggy. I felt that my content lacked focus, as did my form. One question brought clarity to both: "Nate, who is your audience?"

At first, I thought it was my congregants. Knowing that my sermon was going online, I then thought that this spanned the general public. Then it hit me. My primary audiences were the people who had both the knowledge to answer my questions and the power to reform the entire field of biotechnology. The CEO of Monsanto—the head of the largest producer of genetically modified foods in the world—was the perfect person to address my questions to, and the form of an open letter was the perfect way to deliver the sermon. At that minute, my content sharpened. I narrowed the literature into seven questions, and began the sermon as follows:

November 10, 2009
Mr. Hugh Grant
Chairman, President, Chief Executive Officer
Monsanto Company
800 N. Lindbergh Blvd.
St. Louis, MO 63167 USA

Dear Mr. Grant,
The following letter was publicly read aloud on November 1, 2009, at the First Unitarian Universalist Church of Philadelphia, established by Joseph Priestley in 1796, whose discoveries laid the foundation for modern chemistry. Because of his work, we pride ourselves on using science to guide our spiritual and ethical lives. We are a religious people who believe in responsibly participating in the interdependent web of existence of which we are all a part. We are an inquiry-driven people who believe in each person's free and responsible search for truth and meaning.
My letter has seven parts, each dedicated to asking you a moral question about Monsanto's relationships. The first question concerns farmers; the second, your relationship with consumers; the third, your relationship with the media; the fourth, your relationship with universities; the fifth, your relationship with governments; the sixth, your relationship with creation; and the seventh, your relationship with your conscience. The letter closes with a simple request that we meet to publicly discuss these questions in person. I will begin with your relationship to the stewards of the land.

The full sermon, titled "Sovereign Seeds" (Appendix E), included dozens of footnotes. I wanted to make clear to Mr. Grant that we were not a wing-nut religious group. Unitarian Universalists are intellectually curious and open to the use of reason and science.
To ensure that my facts were grounded, I invited members of the ethical eating class to help refine the questions. In addition, Jennifer Hurley and Tricia Way and Ginni Stiles were particularly

helpful as my worship associates and personal spiritual trainers. Both had been trustees of the church and had an intellectual interest in the subject of genetically modified foods. We rehearsed the sermon on Thursday night and discovered that I still needed to refine the content. By Saturday afternoon it was ready.

To my relief, the lengthy sermon held people's attention. During hospitality hour, a first-time visitor joked with me, "It's not as if you're actually going to send the letter to Monsanto." I said to her, "Of course I am. And if I don't get a reply, I will give him a call." She cracked up, to which I said, "What we do here is not a game."

The next day, I sent the letter via FedEx and uploaded the text and podcast to my website. The following week the visitor made a hefty financial contribution to the church. In the weeks following, I started to receive communication from Michael Pollan, author of *In Defense of Food* and *The Omnivore's Dilemma,* and from Robert Kenner, director of the movie *Food, Inc.* I also heard from leaders of the Union of Concerned Scientists, the Center for Food Safety, and the Midwest Coalition for Responsible Investment.

By Thanksgiving, Monsanto replied. I received a thoughtful letter from Diane Herndon, an executive of corporate responsibility. She responded generally to my questions, urging me to review some alternate sources. To my surprise, she closed the letter by inviting us to St. Louis to a meeting with her and her colleagues. We accepted. We set the date for late January.

A month earlier, I led a training seminar for regional social justice leaders. I explained that Unitarian Universalists are particularly effective at being first responders to oppressive agendas. However, I told them, "If we want to build a relevant, prophetic, liberal religion, then we cannot solely base our public actions on the reactions to oppressive agendas. We must not only ask, *What are we against?* We must boldly communicate *what we are for.*" I then asked my colleagues whether they were ready to use their congregations "to train the next generation of first responders to oppressive agendas to be *the* ethical agenda setters of our time."

Later that night, I reread "Sovereign Seeds" and noticed that I was not effectively putting into practice what I preached to my colleagues. Toward the end of the sermon there were some interesting ideas about developing a *Wikiseed* and a code of ethics for the field of biotechnology. These proposed solutions, as written, were parenthetical to the central purpose of that sermon. I realized that I had put them center stage by composing another letter, which served as a way to prepare myself to meet with Monsanto's executives. I treated the second sermon as a discernment process—a way to publicly work out intentions by asking the community to help clarify my talking points.

I entered a worship arts meeting with Trisha Way, who eventually joined me in traveling to St. Louis. We agreed that we knew what we were against, but were not necessarily clear about what we were for. Upon our arrival at Monsanto's headquarters, what specific request would we make of Mr. Grant? What did we expect him to do, really? Would our request be feasible? Would it be measurable? Would it be compelling enough to capture his imagination?

I told Trisha that I had seen too many activists finally get to a table of power only to mistake requests for demands, and invitations for accusations. I was determined to be an effective communicator. I wanted to get clear about why I was there and what I was asking of them. I did not want to spend my time there reacting to whatever agenda I perceived to be oppressive. I wanted to come setting a positive, forward-thinking ethical agenda by using a collegial and inviting tone. I was determined to make a request that was challenging yet realistic—bold and simple—a request for Monsanto to accept, deny, or counter.

Trisha and I knew that we had to make this process public by inviting others into the conversation. That is why, on the day I presented the second sermon, we also advertised a "talkback session"—meaning that after I had delivered the sermon, members of the congregation were able to come to the microphones and present their own thoughts about the ethics of genetically modified foods. We wanted to galvanize the entire community in the process of preparing us for the trip. We were thrilled to see that a dozen people came to the service prepared with powerfully poignant questions. Not everyone agreed, but everyone was engaged. I consider that service to be one of my greatest preaching accomplishments. I felt proud that the entire church was focused on something of significance. For a moment, they moved beyond their own preoccupations and were collectively researching an extremely complicated moral dilemma.

I chose a title for this second sermon in the spirit of articulating, not what I was against, but what I was for: "Monsanto's 21st Century Oath: Do No Harm." (For a video recording, see www. ExorcisingPreaching.com.) I used the sermon as a public invitation for Mr. Grant to join me in meeting with a group of interfaith clergy and bioethicists to craft a twenty-first-century Hippocratic Oath for the entire field of biotechnology. The fact is that this emerging field, unlike the well-established field of medicine, does not have a unified code of ethics. For this reason, I wanted to put into motion something that could outlast us all—principles to guide generations of biotechnicians. To do this, I turned to the literature of biomedical ethics. I was curious as to whether the three primary principles associated with the Hippocratic Oath could serve as scaffolding for the field of biotechnology.

In my sermon, I explained that the first principle, *nonmaleficence*, refers to the philosophy of Hippocrates, the father of Western medicine, whose writings charge medical professionals to *do no harm*. In other words, at times it can be wiser to do nothing than to do something that may cause more harm than good.

I proceeded to describe the second principle, *beneficence*: the moral obligation to act for the benefit of others. I complimented Monsanto on having already produced a public statement to this effect. One of Monsanto's pledges was to "use sound and innovative science and thoughtful and effective stewardship to deliver high-quality products that are *beneficial* to our customers and to the environment."

Building on their pledge, I explained that Monsanto had already demonstrated the intent to implement a third ethic: *distributive justice*. When applied to the pursuit of doubling the yield of their core crops over the next two decades, Monsanto's goal of "feeding the world's hungry" could manifest if they helped to ensure the fair, equitable, and appropriate distribution of food. I said that by making the pledge to practice nonmaleficence, beneficence, and distributive justice, Mr. Grant had the opportunity to lead not only his company but also the entire field of biotechnology in creating a twenty-first-century oath. In appealing to the CEO's own legacy, I suggested that we name it after him.

I said, "Imagine the unveiling of The Grant Oath calling those who produce genetically modified foods to consider the possible harm that any pursuit of scientific advancement may have on people, animals, or the environment. Imagine if Mr. Grant were to leave this enduring legacy to humanity, inviting his colleagues to join him in affirming the following draft pledge:

> I promise to use my expertise
> to help and not harm
> people, animals, and the environment.

> I promise to practice responsibly
> the ancient ethic of stewardship
> and the modern principle of sustainability
> by affirming distributive justice
> as a moral obligation
> to benefit the interdependent web of existence
> of which we are a part.

I used the sermon to explain how each phrase in this draft was connected with the three principles of bioethics. This public exercise gave Trisha and I a clear question to ask each individual executive at Monsanto: "Will you sign this oath?" Our request was simple. It was feasible and compelling. If they said "Yes," we could then ask for the signatures of executives at DuPont and Syngenta. If they said "No," we could ask them to help redraft the oath. Which phrases did they affirm, and which ones made them uncomfortable and why? What language would better represent their values?

I was pleased to see that this strategy was incredibly effective. What began as a two-hour meeting resulted in four days of meetings with over fourteen executives. We met with the director of global development partnership and the vice president for public policy, and we talked over the phone with a research director in Bangalore, India. We talked with the director of human rights and the director of global scientific affairs. We were also invited to Monsanto's annual shareholder meeting, where we met with Mr. Grant and members of Monsanto's board of trustees, including Janice Fields, the chief operating officer of McDonald's.

It was an invigorating process. I document the experience in a third sermon titled "Ministry with Monsanto" (Appendix F). This public annotation of our conversations was published in preparation for our community to welcome two executives from Monsanto who agreed to fly to Philadelphia to have dinner with church leaders. They were so pleased with our initial experience that they agreed to meet members of our congregation. This, too, was a rewarding experience. Our denominational magazine, *UU World,* published an article about the encounter, titled "Dinner with Monsanto" (Appendix G).

❖

I share the intricacies of these results to illustrate the following points. By liberating myself from the notion that all sermons must utilize the same mode of delivery, I was free to create a multifaceted container from which to deliver complex questions in the form of an open letter. This letter resulted in a focused conversation, not only for our community, but also for leaders of a controversial multinational corporation. This conversation, as documented in the appendices, helped advance the moral and intellectual development of church members as well as executives and trustees at Monsanto. Our congregation learned that it is possible for our worship services to inspire those *within* and *beyond* the walls of the sanctuary to *scribe worth*, to *etch meaning*. The religious education classes, the sermons, the talkbacks, and the visits with leaders of Monsanto became opportunities for our church community to collaborate as a single, integrated, and dynamic entity.

Put simply, our yearlong engagement with Monsanto enabled us to *lead by being*. Rather than acting on the impulse to be the interrogator, we generated visions larger than ourselves. When we felt the impulse to be enraged, we accepted the invitation to be empathetic and to no longer make any single person or corporation the object of our aggression and loathing. When we felt the inclination to become liberal fundamentalists, we challenged one another to be curious. When we felt the impulse to be righteous, we transformed our soapbox into a music box and dared to be powerfully playful.

Benediction

The exorcisms listed in this book are not the first, nor the final word. They are invitations for my colleagues to continue to treat preaching as a disciplined spiritual practice. The ultimate goal is that we support each another in liberating ourselves from everything that harms others and ourselves. Two of the many ways this can be achieved is, first, if clergy form local preaching collaboratories and, second, if they submit their exorcisms as draft chapters to be included in the next volume of this series.

A preaching collaboratory is an educational laboratory where religious professionals can collaboratively experiment with preaching techniques. Quarterly or biannually, preachers will organize themselves into small groups to reflect upon the habits that are working for them and to hold one another accountable for purging the habits that are not. They should begin by creating a covenant that reflects their values and the promises they intend to make for one another. They will agree how many times they will meet, and how they will treat one another and hold one another responsible for their commitments. These ground rules will set the tone for their continued collaboration. The purpose is to treat the preaching laboratory as a forum for rigorous self-analysis and theological reflection about the power and potential of preaching. As they meet regularly to test their exorcisms, they will co-create a circle of collegial support, with the awareness that we are not isolated beings. We are intimately connected to one another through the privilege of designing timely and timeless worship.

As these collaboratories form, my hope is that preachers will archive their insights and write them up as draft chapters to be included in the next volume of *Exorcising Preaching*. The submissions may be from a range of topics: from preparing to performing sermons, to the theological assumptions that drive our craft. My hope is that the *Exorcising Preaching* series will help harness the liberating practices of preachers across religious traditions. By submitting their insights to www.ExorcisingPreaching.com, they will enter into the collegial dialogue on the principle that "All of us are smarter than any one of us."

❖

In closing, I have learned that exorcising preaching is a self-induced act of emancipation. It comes with many rewards. When a liberated preacher reflects back the questions and experiences of the people, congregants begin the collective work of scribing meaning, of etching for themselves some sense of honesty, some sense of self-worth. Rather than the religious leader being the sole voice of morality, the preacher and the people collectively treat one another as personal spiritual trainers, each responsible for the care of each other. Together, they exorcise the sentimental and dispel pretense.

The truth is that people will travel across lands to find a truly liberating community. As huddled masses, they will come to the sanctuary to be restored and to do the work of being made whole again. In that space, the people will listen to that which is *within* and *beyond* them and ultimately experience interdependence.

By the end of an intellectually honest and liberating service the worshipers will leave their pews feeling challenged and alive. The struggles of the week ahead may fatigue them, but once again they will return to the sanctuary like trains to the roundhouse. Stories and song, food and fire, will become the means by which they unload their burdens, retool themselves, and turn one another around. They will hear the words of poets, ethicists, artists, and mourners. Preachers will join them in singing of exile, and together they will experience stillness and silence. In this exchange, the people and the preachers will find refuge in the mutual promise that they are not isolated beings but intimately bound to one another and to all that is holy.

References

Chapter 2

Mark Belletini, "A Kol Nidrei," in *Sonata for Voice and Silence: Meditations* (Boston: Skinner House Press, 2008), 22–23.

Rosemary Bray McNatt, "To pray without apology: What would have happened if Martin Luther King Jr. had cast his lot with the Unitarian Universalists? A reflection on race and theology." *UU World*, Boston: Unitarian Universalist Association, November/December 2002.

V. Chapman-Smith, "Stop 24: First Unitarian Church of Philadelphia, 10th and Locust, Philadelphia (original location)," on the audio tour, *John Brown's Philadelphia*. National Archives, Philadelphia.

Horace Howard Furness, "Historical Address delivered in Connection with the Installation of the Reverend Charles E. St. John as Minister of the First Unitarian Church of Philadelphia, 12th of January, 1908," in Horace Howard Furness Jr., ed., *The Letters of Horace Howard Furness* (Boston: Houghton Mifflin, 1922), 102–103.

William Henry Furness, "A sermon occasioned by the destruction of Philadelphia Hall: and delivered the Lord's day following, May 20, 1838, in the First Congregational Unitarian Church" (Philadelphia: J. C. Clark, 1838).

William Henry Furness, "The moving power. A discourse delivered in the First Congregational Unitarian Church in Philadelphia, Sunday morning, Feb. 9, 1851, after the occurrence of a fugitive slave case" (Philadelphia: Merrihew and Thompson, printers, 1851).

William Henry Furness, "A discourse occasioned by the Boston fugitive slave case: Delivered in the First Congregational Unitarian Church, Philadelphia, April 13, 1851." (Philadelphia: Merrihew and Thompson, printers, 1851).

Elizabeth M. Geffen, *William Henry Furness: Philadelphia Antislavery Preacher* (Philadelphia: Historical Society of Pennsylvania, 1958).

William Still, *The Underground Railroad* (New York: Arno Press, 1968), 633. (Originally published in Philadelphia: Porter & Coates, 1872).

Chapter 6

Sheryl Prenzlau, *The Jewish Children's Bible: Exodus*, illustrated by Zely Smekhov and Lena Guberman (New York: Pitspopany Press, 1997).

Chapter 7

Connie Simon, *How Do I Love Someone Seemingly Unlovable?* a Call to Worship delivered at First Unitarian Church of Philadelphia on October 2, 2011.

Principles and Sources of Unitarian Universalism

Unitarian Universalism is a religion with deep roots in the Christian tradition, going back to the Reformation and beyond—to early Christianity. Over the last two centuries our sources have broadened to include a spectrum ranging from Eastern religions to Western scientific humanism. Unitarian Universalists identify with and draw inspiration from Atheism and Agnosticism, Buddhism, Christianity, Humanism, Judaism, Earth-Centered Traditions, Hinduism, Islam, and more. Many Unitarian Universalists have grown up in these traditions—some have grown up with no religion at all. Unitarian Universalists may hold one or more of those traditions' beliefs and practice its rituals.

Unitarian Universalist congregations together affirm and promote seven Principles and are guided by six Sources. The following statement grew out of the grassroots of our communities, was affirmed democratically, and serves as a guide for those who choose to join and participate in Unitarian Universalist communities.

We, the member congregations of the Unitarian Universalist Association, covenant to affirm and promote

- The inherent worth and dignity of every person;
- Justice, equity and compassion in human relations;
- Acceptance of one another and encouragement to spiritual growth in our congregations;
- A free and responsible search for truth and meaning;
- The right of conscience and the use of the democratic process within our congregations and in society at large;
- The goal of world community with peace, liberty and justice for all;
- Respect for the interdependent web of all existence of which we are a part.

The living tradition which we share draws from many sources:

- Direct experience of that transcending mystery and wonder, affirmed in all cultures, which moves us to a renewal of the spirit and an openness to the forces which create and uphold life;
- Words and deeds of prophetic women and men which challenge us to confront powers and structures of evil with justice, compassion and the transforming power of love;
- Wisdom from the world's religions which inspires us in our ethical and spiritual life;
- Jewish and Christian teachings which call us to respond to God's love by loving our neighbors as ourselves;
- Humanist teachings which counsel us to heed the guidance of reason and the results of science, and warn us against idolatries of the mind and spirit;
- Spiritual teachings of Earth-centered traditions which celebrate the sacred circle of life and instruct us to live in harmony with the rhythms of nature.

Grateful for the religious pluralism, which enriches and ennobles our faith, we are inspired to deepen our understanding and expand our vision. As free congregations we enter into this covenant, promising to one another our mutual trust and support. [12]

Appendix B

Justified

Nathan C. Walker

Preached at the First Unitarian Church of Philadelphia on Sunday, October 21, 2013 in response to the musical Parade *produced by the Arden Theater Company.*

In Atlanta, Georgia, precisely one hundred years ago, a child laborer was found dead in the basement of a pencil factory. Mary Phagan, a thirteen-year old girl, was found with a seven-foot cord wrapped around her neck; her dress was found flipped-up around her waist and her petticoat torn off; her skull had been bruised, her face blackened, and dirt and ash from the floor were pressed into her open wounds. Mary Phagan was thirteen years old. She worked 55 hours a week for $4.05 cents. A sweet little girl: respectful and hardworking. She had an angelic face.

On the day of the annual memorial parade, Mary Phagan went to the pencil factory to ask the superintendent for her pay. While the rest of Atlanta was preparing for commemorating veterans, the superintendent was in his office, up on the third floor. By the time Mary Phagan met the superintendent, the office boy had already been dismissed, leaving the janitor as the only other person in the building. Mary met with the superintendent, received her money and left; the janitor clocked out, and the superintendent locked up the building. Later that night, the watchman discovered the body of Mary Phagan and called the home of the superintendent. He did not pick up. If he wasn't at home, where could he be? The watchman called the police, and they investigated the crime scene.

The next morning, the police met the superintendent at his home. He was fidgety. He kept ringing his hands. His eyes were shifty, and he kept asking rapid, suspicious questions. The police took him to the crime scene. When asked about the janitor's timesheet, he said everything looked accurate. Later, the superintendent changed his story, saying that the janitor, a black man, had tampered with the punch card. Why did the superintendent change his story? The

103

janitor said he had seen the superintendent carrying Mary Phagan's body. Who should we believe? In 1913, whose story should the Atlanta police have trusted—a "Negro" or a man from one of the wealthiest families in Atlanta?

At the trial, the superintendent was represented by the best lawyer money could buy, whereas the janitor had a court-appointed defense attorney. The mother of Mary Phagan wept as she testified that her daughter had been missing, and she identified the mangled dress. The janitor testified against the superintendent with great poise. He was calm and consistent in his story. A parade of little girls from the pencil factory spoke of the superintendent's sexual advances and shady character. Even his own maid testified against his character—can you imagine how dangerous it must have been for a Negro woman to testify against her boss? When the superintendent finally took the stand, he spoke for three hours about how he runs his business and how he keeps his books, showing the jury his accounting practices—three hours of minutia before he even once mentioned the death of little Mary Phagan. He did not show remorse. Throughout the trial, he was sweating, wringing his hands, and shifting his eyes back and forth. Acting as the prosecutor, the solicitor general urged the jury to find him guilty. The jury agreed, leading the trial judge to sentence the superintendent to death.

The wealthy family that owned the pencil factory paid for the superintendent to go through thirteen appeals. In fact, the case went all the way to the U.S. Supreme Court—even the highest court in the land, in a 7 to 2 ruling, found that the superintendent had had a fair trial. The death penalty would have to stand. And here's where it gets politically and legally complicated.

The governor of Georgia, having been overtly influenced by the superintendent's wealthy family, granted him clemency. Meaning, rather than put him to death, the superintendent's sentenced was changed to life residence on a beautiful "prison farm" in the rolling hills of Georgia, complete with a phonograph and food service— luxuries that poor Mary Phagan had never had in her short life. In outrage over the governor's politicized decision, the trial judge worked with prominent government authorities throughout the state to remove the superintendent from the luxurious prison farm. In front of distinguished elected officials, the trial judge ceremonially read aloud the original sentence. These statesmen lynched him and the superintendent was dead. Citizens throughout the rolling hills of Georgia respected this act of justice. Finally, Mary Phagan was vindicated and could rest in peace.

That's the story. Can you believe the superintendent thought he could get away with such a brutal act and blame it on his black janitor? It's sickening. Some people think they are "justified" to buy their way through the legal system.

Let me ask you this: how many of you have never in your lives heard anything about the story of Mary Phagan? [A supermajority of the congregation raised their hands.] I am surprised because it is one of the most famous murder cases in U.S. history. Its fame comes from the fact that the trial judge would not stand for the governor overturning his decision, let alone the decision of thirteen appeals' courts and the decision of the U.S. Supreme Court. You see, this is a story about checks and balances. It is a story about how in the United States of America no man is above the law—whether that man is an elite superintendent or a corrupt governor—no one should have that much power. It is undemocratic. It is un-American. This is a story of how the will of the people was met with the conviction of their elected leaders to maintain the innocence—the purity—of justice.

Now, how many of you *have* heard of these events? Maybe you learned of them by reading one of the seven books about it or by watching one of the four films or three plays, such as the musical *Parade*. Or maybe you studied this case in your civics or history or law classes.

If you are familiar with these events, then you know that the superintendent's name was Leo Frank, a Jewish man born in Texas and when he was three months old his parents moved to Brooklyn, New York, where he was raised. He was an awkward, reclusive man, standing 5'6" and weighing 120 pounds. Leo Frank married a woman named Lucille Selig, whose uncle found him a job at the family's pencil factory. Leo Frank resented having to be in the South and refused to speak with a Southern drawl. Georgians saw him as a Yankee outsider, a Jew, and a boss to poor white Southerners.

On this fateful day of April 26, 1913, Leo Frank went to work at the pencil factory because he was not about to attend the Confederate Memorial Day Parade. He refused to bemoan the South loosing the Civil War. Yet, despite this political climate, Atlanta had become the industrial gateway to the South, welcoming many immigrants. During the reconstruction period, the Jewish immigrant population in Atlanta had increased from 600 to 3,000. As a result, there were street signs and postings in front of stores that read, "Christians Only," "Jews Not Allowed," and "Applications from Hebrews not desired." These anti-Semitic campaigns were based on the fear that Jews wanted to, quote, "sacrifice Christians for their blood."

During the trial, the prosecution spoke of Leo Frank having previously undergone a ritual circumcision, evidence that he was, quote, "a sexual deviant." Newspapers used this information to characterize Leo Frank as a villain when alleging, "Mary Phagan [was] pursued and tempted, and entrapped, and then killed when she would not do what so many other girls had done for this Jewish hunter of Gentile girls." In upset over similar gross characterizations, Leo Frank's mother erupted from the courtroom bench and tried to swat the prosecutor while shouting. Although "her exact words [were] uncertain...it was widely reported that she called [the prosecutor] a 'Gentile dog' or a 'Christian dog.'" This confirmed the jury's suspicion that Jews could not be trusted.

Before the trial started, a white Christian allegedly said to the judge, "I am glad they indicted the God damn Jew. They ought to take him out and lynch him, and if I get on that jury, I'll hang that Jew, sure." He was selected to serve on the jury. Similarly, before taking the stand, a key witness was overheard saying, "The dam Jew, they ought to hang him."

When investigating the crime, the Atlanta police found a series of notes written from the perspective of Mary Phagan. It was as if she had been writing the notes while she was being raped, which described her perpetrator in detail as being a Negro man. While in custody, the police made the janitor hand write the content of notes and discovered that the original matched the janitor's handwriting. This led them to believe that the janitor wrote the notes with the intent to cast suspicion on another black man whose features significantly differed from his own. During an interrogation, the solicitor general allegedly asked the janitor a leading question: whether Leo Frank forced him to write these notes. With that question, the lead suspect was transformed into the lead witness.

During the trial, the janitor wore a brand new suit. He had shaved, and his hair was freshly cut—all at the cost of the solicitor general. The janitor kept using the same phrases, indicating that he, just like many of the other witnesses, had been coached on what to say. At one point, Leo Frank's attorney asked why there were repeated grammatical errors in the notes that matched the janitor's handwriting—the word "done" was used multiple times when it should have said "did." If Leo Frank had forced him to write the notes, how could he have dictated the exact speech and grammar patterns used by the janitor himself?

After the trial, the janitor's own defense attorney pieced together the transcripts and noted that the janitor had used the term "done" numerous times while testifying. This attorney then published a 100-page study of factual inconsistencies in the janitor's testimony and publicly proclaimed that he thought the janitor had killed Mary Phagan. This was quite odd because he had spent his career defending black clients with great conviction of their innocence. The defense attorney received death threats from his white neighbors, and his entire family was run out of town. At the age of 79, on his death bed, the defense attorney wrote, "I believe in the innocence and good character of Leo M. Frank."

Seventy years after the trial, the young office boy who had worked at the pencil factory signed an affidavit admitting to seeing the janitor "carrying the limp body of Mary Phagan on his shoulder, positioned as if getting ready to dump Phagan down the 2-foot by 2-foot scuttle hole trapdoor next to the elevator. The janitor allegedly…said to the young boy, 'If you tell anyone, I will kill you.'" In addition, Leo Frank's maid confessed that during an extreme police interrogation, the solicitor general compelled her to testify against her boss. Of the parade of little girls who testified against Leo Frank, none of them had ever been alone with him, none of the girls said he had touched them, and the only office girl who allegedly had a complaint refused to testify.

The trial of Leo Frank was the longest in Georgia's history. It ended when the solicitor general choreographed his closing statements by saying the word "guilty" twelve times in perfect sync with the ringing of the neighboring church bell: Guilty! Gong! Guilty! Gong—twelve times. The white folk of Atlanta interpreted this as a divine sign of Leo Frank's guilt. Within two hours, the jury, consisting of twelve white, Christian men, found him guilty. The trial judge sentenced him to be hanged in the public square. Atlanta erupted into celebration, physically carrying the solicitor general above their heads as thousands of people cheered and hung from the windows of buildings waving their Confederate flags.

During the appeals process, which lasted two years, *The New York Times,* owned by a prominent Jewish family, began to investigate the case. Southerners fiercely resented the intervention of the Yankee media. The *Times* reported that in response to some jurors' expressing doubts about the case, they had received death threats. It was also reported that the pastor of Mary Phagan's church said, "One old Negro would be poor atonement for the life of this innocent girl. But when on that next day, the police arrested a Jew, and a Yankee Jew at that, all of the inborn prejudice against Jews rose up in a feeling of satisfaction, that here would be a victim worthy to pay for the crime."

The outgoing governor of Georgia was convinced that it was important to investigate the case, in part, because of the persistence of Leo Frank's wife, Lucille, but also because he had received a number of petitions from Georgia attorneys. In comparing the crime scene with the trial transcripts and seeing that there was nothing but circumstantial evidence and fabricated testimonies, the governor ultimately decided to grant Leo Frank clemency. Within hours of his decision, the governor's mansion was mobbed with rioters. They erected an effigy—a strawman hung from a post with a sign that labeled the governor "The King of the Jews."

While Leo Frank was at the Georgia State Penitentiary, the prison farm, a fellow inmate cut Leo Frank's throat but failed to kill him. Days later, in the middle of the night, the trial judge and twenty-five armed men—consisting of state legislators, judges, and a former governor—kidnapped Leo Frank and drove him to a field opposite Mary Phagan's home. They called themselves the Vigilance Committee. The trial judge ceremoniously read aloud the original sentence, and feeling justified to carry out the will of the people, the members of the committee lynched Leo Frank. Lynching was a common practice: during the Reconstruction period, over 2,800 lynching were reported in the South, with 500 in Georgia. What was uncommon about this lynching is that thousands of white people came to see for themselves Leo Frank's body hanging from the noose—the only Jewish person to be lynched in the United States. Meanwhile, hundreds of black men had been hanging from the trees without any fanfare.

The local newspaper read, "In putting the Sodomite murderer to death, the Vigilance Committee has done what the Sherriff should have done, if [the governor] had not been in the mold of Benedict Arnold. LET JEW LIBERTINES TAKE NOTICE! Georgia is not for sale to rich criminals." This same newspaper called for the revival of the Ku Klux Klan. Within days, scores of men in white cloaks set ablaze a giant wooden cross atop Stone Mountain. The Klan resurrected itself, vowing to protect the "Southern way of life" against blacks, Jews, Catholics, and immigrants. They called themselves the "Knights of Mary Phagan."

If all you knew were the first version of these events, would you, too, be justified to sentence a man to death? The first story is one of vindication—prominent citizens working together to enact their understanding of vigilante justice. The second story is one of group hysteria, fueled by anti-Semitism, xenophobia, Confederate resistance to Yankee privilege, impoverished people rising up against Leo Frank, a so-called immigrant proletariat, whose lynching sparked the resurrection of the Ku Klux Klan in Georgia.

The effects of this tragedy continue to unfold to this day. In response to Leo Frank's arrest, the Anti-Defamation League was founded in 1913—one hundred years ago—under the mission to "stop the defamation of the Jewish people and to secure justice and fair treatment to all." Fast forward to 1986: the Georgia Board of Pardons and Paroles granted Leo Frank "a posthumous pardon based on the state's failure to ensure his safety, but the pardon did not officially exonerate Leo Frank of the murder." In 2009, the descendants of Mary Phagan joined with the descendants of Leo Frank's lynching party to reverently recount the extreme injustice faced by Leo Frank. A descendant of one of the lynchers, Roy Barnes said, "It's a terrible blot on our history… How we keep it from happening again is to never forget."

Why is this a critical event for us to study today? It is a pertinent reminder that none of us are exempt from doing what the white Protestant establishment did in Atlanta one hundred years ago. To know this is true, all we have to do is look at the true nature of the family, the government, and of religion.

How many times have families been broken apart by some faction in the clan feeling justified in taking action against another? Last night, we were recounting the story of how my grandmother's Mormon father did not speak to her for seven years because she married a Catholic man. My great-grandfather felt justified to be a hero to his own story by disowning his own child. This was made possible because he had cast himself as both the victim and the hero in his own story. None of us are exempt from this pattern. Our justifications are constantly bound by the ideologies from which they stem. We become so justified that we construct a narrative that reinforces our intent to see what we want to see, keeping us from seeing that we are actually causing another harm.

Is that not what's replaying in the government today? Leaders feel justified to shut the government down. They feel justified to take justice into their own hands and to circumvent an entire legal system. This is made possible when people are indoctrinated by one particular set of news sources, casting themselves as the heroes of their own story.

Take, for instance, the recent poll that found that people opposed to Obamacare had favored the Affordable Care Act. They did not know that it is the same thing. How is it that those who have been so ideologically opposed to Obamacare were a part of the group that initially proposed the idea? How is it that those who would benefit most from universal health care have been led to believe they should oppose it?

In 2013, the so-called United States are bound by the remnants of the ideological dualism that played out in the Civil War. One side sees its actions as patriotic and just, whereas the other deems such actions as irrational, exclusionary, and discriminatory. All of this is made possible when one tribe in one territory draws upon one particular set of sources. One tribe's members cast a narrative that leads them to be the victims and the heroes in their own stories.

The only way out of this delusion is to expand our circle of sources. This begins by drawing more on doubt than on certainty. We ask ourselves, are we sure? How about this idea? What does this person think or feel? How about from this perspective? In time, we begin to train ourselves to be curious. When doing so, we become less and less convinced that our unexamined assumptions reveal the totality of reality. We achieve this goal when we expand our circle of sources.

How many religions in how many civilizations bound themselves to one particular source text constructed by one particular set of teachers in on particular point in time? Methodologically, this is flawed. It is designed for people throughout their history to restrict themselves to one type of human experience. At best, people spend a lifetime going deep into one culture. I am all for depth, but it cannot be at the cost of being ignorant to breadth.

By expanding our circle of sources, we begin to expand our worldview, our capacity to understand—and understanding need not imply agreement. What do we do here week after week? We expand our circle of sources. One week, we'll draw upon the wisdom in one of the world's religions, and the next, we'll draw from the direct experience of a Jewish man who was lynched in 1915. The next week, we'll practice how to dethrone ourselves from the center of the world, calling ourselves to replace the belief that all of this was made for our consumption with beliefs that inspire us to be stewards of this vast interdependent web of which we are a part.

We are an intentionally diverse community designed to expand our circle of sources so that none of us become bound by the idolatries of the mind or spirit. We come not to experience a social club that will reinforce our own beliefs. We come to this place as a moral training ground to challenge us to see that we are not exempt from oppressive systems; we are immoral agents with the great moral capacity to emancipate ourselves from the harm we help to create. Until then, none of us will be free.

Week after week, religions throughout the world are trying to save our souls. In here, we come to save our character. We come to expand our circle of sources. We want to learn more from our family members, our neighbors, and especially from those with whom we disagree. In doing so, we practice how to question whether we have the full story. This aids us each time we read the news and each time we enter the voting booth. This aids us each time we meet someone familiar or encounter someone different in the town square.

In closing, what great lesson comes from the tragic murder of Mary Phagan and lynching of Leo Frank? It is a lesson that we are trying to learn and relearn week after week. As humans, we are limited. None of us are exempt from having justified harm to another in pursuit of reinforcing our limited truth. This is why we need one another. We need one another to expand our circle of awareness, to push open our circle of compassion. Our justifications are only as strong as the credibility of our information. And our information is only as credible as the complexity of our sources.

Benediction

As we return into to our ideological worlds, let us remember that doubt can cure us, curiosity can redeem us, and intellectual honesty can save us from becoming what we set out against.

APPENDIX C

Are You the 1 Percent?

Nathan C. Walker

Preached at the First Unitarian Church of Philadelphia on December 11, 2011.

Video archive: www.ExorcisingPreaching.com

It was a Sunday: Sunday, November 13th. And from this pulpit I spoke these words in a sermon titled, *Leading by Being.*

> We, as one strong body, are required to lead by being. When we feel the impulse to be the interrogator we must choose to be the generator of visions larger than ourselves. When we feel the impulse to be enraged we must accept the invitation to be empathetic and no longer make people the object of our aggression. When we feel the impulse to be furious let us dare to be curious. When we feel the impulse to be righteous let us transform our soapbox into a music box. Let us dare to be powerfully playful.

Sounds lovely, doesn't it? I shared these words with my congregation in Philadelphia on Sunday. And then... Tuesday rolled around.

I was in New York City to meet my partner for a lecture at New York University. Vikram is really into this series, which asks, "Would the world be better off without religion?" So when asked whether I wanted to join him—a funny question to ask a minister—I said, "Yes, dear."

We arrived an hour and a half early because it was open seating. We were pleased to get the center two seats of the fifth row. My partner was so excited, acting like a little kid, asking, "Do you know about this speaker, and that idea, and this and that?" He was so adorable.

112

Just before the event started he went to the restroom and he put his coat on his seat. A little while later the usher said, "Any empty seats can go to those who haven't yet found one." I told the usher that my partner was in the bathroom. She said, "Yeah, that's okay." She started to assist other people.

Then a woman came to the seat next to me and picked up Vikram's coat. I said, "I'm sorry, that's reserved. He's in the bathroom." She continued to sit down and the man with her, maybe her husband, sat down in the other empty seat.

I said, "I'm sorry, my partner's in the bathroom. This seat is taken."

She remained seated, not saying anything. She stared straight ahead as if pretending not to hear me then passed my partner's coat to the man she was with.

I started to explain again, "I'm sorry, but we have been here for over an hour and a half. We came all the way from Philadelphia." Just then, Vikram started to walk down the aisle. I said, "Look, he's right there."

She replied—and this is where it gets a little crazy. She said, "We sponsored this event."

Okay.

So remember Sunday? Yeah. I said these words: "When we feel the impulse to be enraged we must accept the invitation to be empathetic and no longer make people the object of our aggression."

Well. I did not do that at all. Instead, my response was this, "Oh. You're the 1 percent. I've been wanting to meet you."

I continued, "You say you sponsored this event. Do you own the chair or the whole theater?"

It gets worse. From the aisle, my partner asks, "Where's my coat?"

I looked over to see that the man put it on the ground. Thankfully the people sitting next to him passed the coat to my partner.

I stood and said, "She's a 1percenter—she thinks she owns the joint."

Everyone starts to look at us. The woman's spine became erect, which seemed to add an extra glimmer to her pearls.

I, well—I kept going.

I said, "You must be someone really important. Are you famous? If not, let me help you be."

I took out my phone and started…taking her photo. I said, "I think people should know how you behave in the public square."

I pressed the little camera icon while saying, "I'll entitle this one, *Entitlement.*"

Oh, my god. I can't believe it.

So that's the worst of it.

The lights started going down, and Vikram was already at another seat in the back of the theater. I picked up my things and went to the lobby to speak with the house manager to recount the events. I said, "I want to show you this picture. I'm not going to do anything with it. I just want you to know how your sponsor is treating other patrons." The house manager was very apologetic and responded by offering us season passes to this series. The irony was simply divine.

I returned to the theater and found a seat in the balcony and enjoyed the debates. That's it. That's the end of the story and the start of a completely different journey.

I shared what happened with a member of our congregation, Ranwa Hammamy. She's heading off to seminary and has a vibrant ministry in our community. I showed her the picture and while giggling said, "Look at her face. And look at those behind her, gasping with fear."

Ranwa paused, then asked me a really powerful, spiritually mature question: "Nate, why are you keeping the picture?"

I took pause, then answered her honestly: "Maybe it's pride. I feel wronged and want to gloat." Her question gave me the opportunity to reflect.

I have come to realize that inside of me is a deep-rooted scorecard that rewards me for humiliating people. It cries out like a Master of Ceremonies at a Tuesday Circus, "Step on up, boy, you just got a point for *being* witty. Yes. There you go; here's another for *being* sarcastic. Ding, ding, ding. You showed her."

By many standards my do-justice card was chock full with points.

But here's the thing. That's not my scorecard. My true scorecard is up there, on the pulpit with that Sunday reading. It's the scorecard that is made each time Unitarian Universalists gather to remember why we do justice work in the first place.

I have to be honest. It's really hard for me to earn those kinds of Sunday points when living a Tuesday kind of life. I'm here one day and there another day. I'm in the struggle. I'm in that struggle for an integrated life, where my public words match my private deeds, where my private thoughts mirror my deepest ideals.

The truth is, my impulses don't always spring from kindness. I've been trained to think that kindness is weak. I've been trained to believe that interrogation should be harsh and that rage is always justified. I was trained to believe that justice means storming the castle, screaming at the top of my lungs, "PEACE!"

All that does is make a lot of smoke and ash. Besides, screaming makes my face hurt.

I feel sad and a bit embarrassed to admit it, but it's true. I do not like that part of myself. I do not want to be known for humiliating people. I don't feel good when treating other people this way. It's certainly not the first time something like that has happened. I'm a UU. I know how to spar with someone, especially during church committee meetings.

Why is it so easy for me to become what we set out against? Isn't that the game? The minute we see some injustice, we pounce. I'm sorry. I mean to say, "I pounce." I engage in the role of the Righteous One. I have long since mastered this role. I rehearse it when watching the political pundit, when reading the flaming blog: it's the same ole game, where "success" is built upon demeaning others rather than making meaning of our lives.

If that's true, how is that achieved in this situation? What were my options? To just give her the seat? To quietly sit by and smile nice and talk pretty? I am sharing this story not because there's some scripted answer. I want to include you in the struggle. By all means, tell me, show me, coach me in a new way of playing the justice game. What options were available to me at the time and what options are available to me now?

There is one alternative. Maybe Ranwa's question can help me start playing a new kind of game. It begins by deleting the picture. Yeah. That's a good step. I recently took one last look at the photo and pressed delete. It felt really good.

I want to thank Ranwa for serving as my PST— in our congregation, when someone does something extremely profound, we grant them the title of Personal Spiritual Trainer. She was my PST, a spiritual guide, reminding me of another way of being in the world. That's what we do for one another, week after week. We call one another back into a new kind of game, which grants fulfilling rewards.

You'll be humored to know that months later, my friends were looking at photos on my phone when they found the one of the woman from the theater. I couldn't believe it. I should have known!

After you delete a photo you've got to *take out the trash.*

Damn, isn't that true to life? The things we thought we deleted are not completely erased. Only after we take that second step are we really free from becoming what we set out against. This happens when we return to our spiritual home to experience a new kind of Sunday. Here's another passage from my words shared on that fateful Sunday. It's hard to imagine that these words came from me.

> What does justice-making look like, feel like, when we receive hostile communication? Are we hostile in return? Or is something else required of us? What we choose to do is a reflection of who we believe ourselves to be. It all depends on our beliefs about power.
>
> I once believed it to be powerful to condemn wrongdoers. I believed it right to tear down another's unexamined assumptions and vaporize those whose presence was not worthy of my attention. I believed that others were the cause of my aggression: others were to blame for my feelings of despair, disappointment, and righteousness indignation.
>
> Rather than anger being used as a signal that some-thing was wrong, anger became the solution to all my problems. It felt good to fuel the addiction of righteousness. I was doing justice. I was doing justice. But! I was being an asshole.
>
> I am merely five years into my ministry and have long since mastered the art of being an asshole.
>
> I have spent far too much energy using the public forum as a battlefield. I have spent far too much energy using the public forum to annihilate those perceived to be my enemy. I have armed myself with faithful friends, so that each time we walked into a room, those present would shade their gaze and whisper in dread, "The UUs have arrived."
>
> I used to believe that being feared was powerful. I used to believe it was my duty to free the oppressed, but when reacting with righteous anger, guess who became the oppressor?
>
> Thich Nhat Hahn, a Zen Buddhist, said, "I came to set the prisoner free only to realize the prisoner was me."

So here's the point of this story. I want to use this opportunity to ask a question to all my faithful justice-seeking friends. I want to know from all those who have dedicated their lives to human rights, to civil rights, to environmental justice: What makes Unitarian Universalists uniquely poised to *be* an effective, justice-seeking people? Meaning, what makes our religious movement different than the Occupy Movement or the Freedom to Marry campaign or Amnesty International or any number of secular groups? We are poised to do something uniquely different than the Sierra Club and the United Nations and the World Bank. What is the kernel of our work?

We've seen it in the heart of engaged Buddhists. Their very presence makes us take pause. We've witnessed that quality of being when a Quaker walks into a room. We've seen firsthand the power of what happens when people of faith, who are grounded in reason, inspire one another to higher ground. We need not spend all our energy on doing justice, but, instead, can spend an equal amount on training ourselves to behave in ways that will transform the conflict at hand, not escalate it. We have seen, time and time again, evidence of how kindness need not breed weakness; for if there's any takeaway from my experience, please reflect upon the weaknesses that were inherent in my own impulsive righteousness. How is it that someone who was trained to protect "the other" so easily classified another woman as a 1percenter? I was so worked up by the experience that showing the photo became a kind of trophy. That is, of course, until a fellow Unitarian Universalist kindly showed me a new way.

I believe that Unitarian Universalists know deep in our hearts that it is not only about doing justice, doing justice, doing justice; it's all about *being* kind. It's about modeling for others the behavior we want to see. That's why there is strength found in community. Week after week, gaggles of UUs invite one another into a new kind of game. It's a game that says that my win is not your loss; your failure is not my soapbox; your mistake is not a call for me to be your teacher, your judge, or your bully-pulpit-using preacher. It's not a game that hardens me to all that's wrong in the world. It's a game that softens my heart—that's what our religion requires of us, to soften to one another, time and time again.

So would the world be better off without religion? Absolutely, if it's the kind of religion that is used to harm. But when a religious community is deeply rooted in systems of kindness, generations of people learn how to help make the world better off. We can be such a people, making the message of Unitarian Universalism more and more relevant to this goal of building up the world. We can do this by grounding our faith in everyday practices that invite us into a new way of being in the world. That's what we do week after week: we return to that gaggle of UUs to be reminded that *Standing on the Side of Love* is not a political slogan—it is a way of life.

Each time we gather, someone among us will have the courage to cast a vision. And we'll collectively ask whether such a dream is idealistic or realistic. And a few days later that same person will offer a confession and say, "I totally blew it." We'll respond by saying, "That's what Tuesdays are for—to test our ideals." That's when we reach out a hand, offer a seat, and say, "Let the new game begin." And week after week we find ourselves coming home. We return to our spiritual home, to meet the many Personal Spiritual Trainers who inspire us to reset, to press delete; and who remind us to also take out the trash.

When such exchanges occur, we make it our highest priority to treat one another with the utmost respect. We know the purpose of our religion: the gathered community serves as a training ground—a moral training ground to save us from becoming what we set out against.

When we recount our Tuesday stories, and finally admit our part in fueling the flames, we begin to see a larger pattern. It asks us, "Nate, if you treat a stranger that way, how are you treating your partner? How are you treating your family? Nate, how are you treating yourself?"

When we are held in one another's presence, we give one another permission to be so vulnerable. That's what it means to be called to do Unitarian Universalist justice work. It's not the kind of justice work that makes us hardened to the suffering in the world; the craft itself requires that we soften, more and more each day.

And when we blow it on Tuesday, we may just find refuge in a faith tradition that both nurtures and challenges. We may just find refuge in putting down the torches and choosing not to storm the castle, in putting down the matches and choosing not to fuel the fire.

So, come, lovers of justice and keepers of the dream; come, justified tyrants and suppressers of screams: you are all welcome here. None of us are exempt. We have all played the parts: the peacemaker, the warmonger. They live within.

That is why we, as seekers of freedom, are required to make justice not simply a product but a process: just actions are the means by which to achieve a justice society. When we observe oppression let us develop strategies that free not only the oppressed but also the oppressor. Those who use their power to deny freedom to others are also imprisoned and are also worthy of care. Do not let their unjust actions inspire us to justify employing cruel means, or else we'll soon become what we set out against.

The challenge is this: let us take up the miseducation of justice-making by stripping our conscience of images of equity that claim to manifest through condemnation, through humiliation, through shame and blame and righteous indignation. No. The craft of justice-making begins by marrying a just thought with a kind word, inspiring us to collective action: daring to free both the oppressed and the oppressor, for we know what it's like to be both.

Don't get me wrong—stand we must; stand strong and bold. But in the name of love, let us choose a new kind of game: rather than shoving our foot on the oppressor's neck let us instead reach out a hand, offer a seat, and show them, and even ourselves, a new way of leading by being.

A Letter to My Murderer

Nathan C. Walker

The following sermon was presented at a worship service on Saturday, February 27, 2009, at the General Assembly of Unitarian Universalist Congregations in Salt Lake City, Utah. The first two paragraphs were written with the help of Christine Carlson and Janet Scannel, members of the First Unitarian Church of Philadelphia.

Audio archive: www.ExorcisingPreaching.com

Reader #1

On Sunday, July 27, 2008, Jim David Adkisson walked into the Tennessee Valley Unitarian Universalist Church as twenty-five children and youth performed the musical *Annie*. Adkisson opened a guitar case, pulled out a 12-gauge shotgun, and began firing. Two people were killed: Greg McKendry and Linda Kraeger. Seven more were injured. Adkisson was restrained by three congregation members and one visitor for three minutes before the police department responded to the 911 call. Adkisson's ex-wife had been a member of the Tennessee Valley Church in the 1990s, but was not currently a member of the congregation. Adkisson's hatred of liberalism, including his hatred for the church's acceptance of homosexuality, was expressed in a letter found by police. In an affidavit, one of the police officers who interviewed Adkisson said, "During the interview, Adkisson stated that he had targeted members of the church because of its liberal teachings and his belief that all liberals should be killed because they were ruining the country... [H]e felt that the Democrats had tied his country's hands in the war on terror and...had ruined every institution in America with the aid of major media outlets. Adkisson stated that because he could not get to the leaders of the liberal movement that he would then target those who had voted them into office." Adkisson had also stated that he intended to keep firing until the police killed him. It did not get to that point because members of the congregation tackled him and held him until the police arrived. He was given the right to legal representation and a fair trial at which time he pleaded guilty to two counts of murder and accepted a life sentence without parole. Unfortunately, he showed no remorse.

Reader #2

In this case, the prosecution, representing the state of Tennessee, decided not to request the death penalty. Tennessee does have the death penalty and has used various methods for imposing it over the years, changing methods roughly every century. In the 1800s Tennessee imposed the death penalty by hanging, in the 1900s by electrocution, and, beginning in the year 2000, by lethal injection. Would Unitarian Universalists be supportive of this type of sentencing? If the members of the Tennessee Valley Unitarian Universalist church are similar to those who took a recent survey at the First Unitarian Church of Philadelphia, then about 13 percent will favor the death penalty in this case. What would those who were in the room during the shooting want? What would the victims' families want? And what would the congregation do? The family and congregation had three options: wait to see what the court would decide, petition the court to impose the death penalty, or petition the court not to impose the death penalty. As we have heard today, some members of our Unitarian Universalist family have experienced the pain of a loved one being murdered. The rest of us cannot truly know how we would react. Would we want vengeance? Would we want mercy? In our time together today, our hope is that we can honor all reactions and opinions. Our hope is that we can find our common humanity, however each of us may define that term, in the complexity of our responses.

[This text was followed by a musical response.]

Sermon

I have designed this sermon as an exercise in the moral imagination; a way for me to picture myself as one who was murdered. By doing so, tenderness, compassion, and empathy may be born from my imagined suffering. My intention is to engage the moral imagination as an everyday spiritual practice by trying to see through the eyes of those who suffer.

My words do not claim to offer lofty promises or absolute answers, but may inspire those who are open to wrestling with the ethics of capital punishment. It may inspire those who have never thought about the complexities of the death penalty, or those who have never taken a public stand on the issue. My hope is that this sermon may help all those present to reframe their beliefs and put their faith into action, aware that the pen can be, as Edward Bulwer-Lytton said, mightier than the sword. We are not powerless. We are powerful agents of conscience.

Let us take up this challenge by first considering a legal model by which, when sentencing a murderer, the courts could take into consideration the wishes of the victim. What would happen if the state respected the wishes of the dead? What comfort could the court bring to the victim's families? Would taking the wishes of murder victims into consideration make a difference? What if we drafted a document to address our own specific beliefs about capital punishment, in order to guide the state and our families in the event that we are ever murdered? What if we literally composed a letter to a hypothetical person who might one day kill us? Could such a letter serve as an advance directive to be used in the courts?

An advance directive tells your doctors the kind of care you wish to have if you are, for example, in a coma and are unable to make medical decisions. It is designed not only to let medical staff know your wishes regarding end-of-life care, but also to advise your family. An advance directive allows your loved ones to know exactly what you would want them to do in a time of crisis. I had the honor of caring for a family recently who faced the necessity of making difficult choices for a parent who had left an advance directive. The advance directive informed doctors that this individual did not wish to be kept alive by machines if the heart could no longer beat or if it was no longer possible to breathe naturally. The doctors were given a DNR order, which stands for "do not resuscitate"; another term used in the field is AND, "allow natural death." Many people long for a natural death and legally craft documents that permit the system to honor their wishes. What if we were to craft advance directives to address the question of capital punishment?

I ask this question in the context of the Knoxville tragedy—the day Jim David Adkisson entered the Tennessee Valley Unitarian Universalist sanctuary on a Sunday morning and opened fire during a children's production. Greg McKendry and Linda Kraeger died that day, while seven others were wounded.

If we could go back in time and ask Greg and Linda to write a letter to their murderer, what would they want to say to him? What statement might they make about his crime and what kind of punishment would they affirm? Could such a statement make a difference?

In the following letter, Jim is the hypothetical name given to my fictitious murderer. My words serve as an advance directive, informing my loved ones and the state of my dying wish. It does so by speaking directly to the person who may take my life. It is designed to be a personal statement of conscience that could be used in any court of law.

❖

June 27, 2009

Dear Mr. Adkisson,

If you are reading this letter, you have taken my life. I am dead. You are alive.

I write this letter without knowing your motives for killing. I also do not know the events in your own life that contributed to your actions.

I do know, however, that my family must be in excruciating pain. I imagine my loved ones, my friends, and members of my community weeping and cursing your name. They are probably asking, "Why did you kill him?" It is likely that some of them want to kill you with their bare hands. They may want revenge.

We may not ever know why you killed me, but this much is true. You must repent. You must confess. You must make amends and sincerely and deeply apologize to my family. This is the right thing to do. Then you must receive your punishment.

Thankfully, we live in a justice-seeking nation. Therefore, you will be granted a fair trial and, if found guilty, will experience severe repercussions. I cannot predict in which jurisdiction your trial will be held, nor what state and federal laws will be in place. I can, however, say that I place my trust in the system.

I believe it is right for the state to do anything in its power to remove you from society so that you will not harm another living being. I believe it is right for the state to do anything in its power to make a bold statement to the world that whoever takes life will receive death. I believe it is just for you to receive capital punishment. No one who takes a life deserves to continue living. I believe we must save society from murderers like you and that, therefore, we must do God's work by sentencing you to death.

My dying wish is that whatever pain you may have caused me, you yourself may experience. My dying wish is that my family members can, if they desire, be present for your execution. Your death will comfort them because they will be able to see for their own eyes that you are no longer in the world.

In fact, I would like your execution to be made public so that all who suffered, all who seek justice, can know that the state lawfully played its part in protecting us all.

After you are dead, you will receive the ultimate punishment. For only God can pass final judgment on your soul. I find comfort in knowing that your soul will be damned, while mine will be made whole.

I wonder if you ever knew love? I wonder if there will be… I wonder… Will this letter…the one composed to you now…will it ever have my signature?

God, give me the strength to sign this letter… God, give me the strength…give me the strength to write another… [*Crumple letter in front of congregation.*]

❖

June 27, 2009

Dear Mr. Adkisson,

If you are reading this letter, you have taken my life. I am dead. You are alive.

You have received a fair trial and were found guilty. The state will inevitably choose an appropriate punishment for you; it is not my role to affirm or deny the court's decision. My faith lies in the system. I know that those in power will do what is right.

I am but the dead—a voiceless victim of the past because you robbed me of my future. I am but the dead—a veiled memory of the past whose life will live on in the memories of my loved ones.

I want to write to them and tell them how much they are loved. From them, I learned patience and kindness. From them, I learned honesty and gratitude. From them, I learned to accept whatever comes. I accept the fact that you are now alive, while I am dead. There is nothing left for me to do. I have no voice.

I am powerless to affect your actions or the system that will chart your future. Fate will decide what happens. It is not for me to say.

It is not my responsibility to do anything… It is not even my responsibility to write this letter. Why give any attention to the one who stripped me of my dignity? You do not deserve to hear from me. Why bother? It is not as if anything I say here will matter anyway… [*Crumple letter in front of congregation.*]

❖

June 27, 2009

Dear Mr. Adkisson,

If you are reading this letter, you have taken my life. I am dead. You are alive.

I may be dead, but my life continues through the memories of my loved ones. My life continues through the legacy of these words. I am aware of my power. I am aware of my responsibility. I am aware that my words may help to determine your fate.

When I think of your future, the writings of my spiritual guides come to mind. I hear my teacher Thich Nhat Hahn say, "I am determined not to kill, not to let others kill, and not to support any act of killing in the world, in my thinking, and in my way of life." I hear Gandhi saying, "An eye for an eye makes the whole world blind."

I am but one human life. I am a man who has made many mistakes; a man who has hurt many. I am not without sin. I have certainly been blinded by rage. Who is to say whether or not my life would have put me in a position in which I felt justified to kill? I suppose this letter puts me in such a situation. I must now say whether I believe that you should live or die.

I have the power to craft an advance directive, condemning you to death. I have the power to make your death my dying wish. My loved ones have the power to seek revenge in the name of justice by asking that you be sentenced to death, but can true justice be achieved through violence? Dr. King said, "Through violence you may murder a murderer, but you can't murder murder. Through violence you may murder a hater, but you can't murder hate. Darkness cannot put out darkness. Only light can do that..."

Where is the light in these dark days? Where is the light found in the belly of my family's grief? I imagine that my loved ones are experiencing excruciating pain, knowing that their Natie has been killed. Yet, their suffering must pale in comparison to the pain your loved ones must be feeling, knowing that you have killed.

I believe that allowing you to live will be the most just punishment. Death is easy. Life? Life is hard.

My dying wish is that you live. You must learn to live with yourself; you must live with the past; you must live with your sentence.

My hope is that the prosecutor or district attorney will not propose capital punishment as a result of my homicide. My hope is that you will receive a fair trial, that the judge and jury will look favorably on my words and that the court will pass a sentence in accordance with my wishes. If not, my hope is that the governor will grant you clemency, and pardon you, removing you from death row. In no way should my statement be read as a wish that you should go unpunished. You should be punished. But how?

I wish for you to be immediately removed from society. I wish that you may have time alone to sit with your thoughts, aware of the power of your mind. As a Hindu proverb once said, your thoughts shape your words, which shape your actions, your habits, your character, and your destiny.

I wish for you to have time with others to help process your thoughts, aware that your actions have shaped your destiny and mine. I wish for adequate resources to be given to you to aid in your eventual rehabilitation. In that time, my hope is that you will be given the responsibility to preserve life.

I want you to be sentenced to tend a garden. I want you to name your plants after those in history who have sought to preserve life—give each plant a name, and teach others about the significance of that name. My hope is that you will do everything in your power to keep these plants alive. In time, those aiding in your rehabilitation may deem you ready to care for another being. When you are truly ready, my wish is that you be entrusted with caring for a cat. I want you to name him Nate. I want you to take care of your new animal companion. Treat him with dignity, just as you seek to preserve your own. Discipline him with care, just as you discipline yourself by practicing self-care. I believe in you.

You may have taken my life, you may have stripped me of my dignity, you may have harmed my loved ones unimaginably, but know that the cycle of violence will not aid in releasing their pain, nor will it bring me back to life. My life will only continue if you preserve the essence of my memory.

Therein lies your charge: to use your power to preserve my memory, to use your power to preserve your dignity, to use your power to preserve life.

I close my letter with some questions for you: What will you do with your new life? What purpose will come from these events? What vision will you craft for yourself?

Just as these questions are asked of you, one question remains for me: Will this letter receive my signature?

Just as this question is asked of me, another remains for those who listen to these words. The question is not which of these three letters will receive my signature. The question is, which of these letters will *you* write?

Appendix E

Sovereign Seeds

Nathan C. Walker

Preached at the First Unitarian Church of Philadelphia on November 1, 2009.

Introduction

As the proverb goes, "When we sow our thoughts, we reap our language; when we sow our language, we reap our actions; when we sow our actions, we reap our habits; when we sow our habits, we reap our character; when we sow our character, we reap our destiny."

In this way, a thought is like a seed. If sown intentionally, a thought can yield language that opens the heart, opens the mind, and, in turn, opens the hand of peace.

The purpose of this sermon is to offer a collegial hand of peace, in the form of a letter, addressed to one of the most influential people in the world. It is a letter that intentionally plants a seed, a seed that, if grown collectively, can heal some of the most critical relationships of our time. This public letter is addressed to Mr. Hugh Grant, the Chairman, President, and Chief Executive Officer of Monsanto, a multinational agricultural biotechnology corporation that produces over ninety percent of the world's genetically engineered seeds,[13] such as soy, corn, and cotton. Monsanto is one of the largest producers of glyphosate herbicides and, because of numerous damaged relationships, has become a controversial enterprise.

A copy of this letter will be sent to leaders of numerous national and international agencies with the intent that the ideas presented here will elicit a public conversation not only about our relationship with one another, but also about our relationship with food. It is urgent that we collaborate in creating a public forum by which we can collectively study one of the most critical moral issues of our time: sovereign seeds.

Public Letter to Mr. Grant

November 10, 2009

Mr. Hugh Grant
Chairman, President, Chief Executive Officer
Monsanto Company800 N. Lindbergh Blvd.
St. Louis, MO 63167 USA

Dear Mr. Grant,

The following letter was publicly read aloud on November 1, 2009, at the First Unitarian Universalist Church of Philadelphia, established by Joseph Priestley in 1796, whose discoveries laid the foundation for modern chemistry. Because of his work, we pride ourselves on using science to guide our spiritual and ethical lives. We are a religious people who believe in responsibly participating in the interdependent web of existence of which we are all a part. We are an inquiry-driven people who believe in each person's free and responsible search for truth and meaning.

My letter has seven parts, each dedicated to asking you a moral question about Monsanto's relationships. The first question concerns farmers; the second, your relationship with consumers; the third, your relationship with the media; the fourth, your relationship with universities; the fifth, your relationship with governments; the sixth, your relationship with creation; and the seventh, your relationship with your conscience. The letter closes with a simple request that we meet to publicly discuss these questions in person. I will begin with the stewards of the land.

Relationship with Farmers

Your company's relationship with farmers is naturally strained: humanity has traveled from localized agrarian societies to the three-pronged junction of the age of industrialization, the age of technology, and the age of globalization. As a result, small farms are being replaced with industrial farms. Natural seeds are being replaced with genetically engineered seeds. Local food production is being replaced with international systems to mass-produce food not only for people, but also for the nonhuman animals produced by those industrial farms.

I understand that two of Monsanto's goals are, one, to genetically modify seeds that will produce plants to withstand the herbicide intended to control area weeds and, two, to genetically engineer seeds that will produce plants that create a higher yield and use less acreage. By patenting the science used to redesign the DNA of a seed, your company legally receives a financial return on its investment.

Patent laws protect your seeds from being duplicated, allowing you the legal right to create use-agreements with farmers that prevent them from reselling the seeds or using the seeds from one harvest for the next. This system has led Monsanto to invest over $10,000,000 annually in a legal team of seventy-five attorneys[14] to litigate those who breach your technology agreements, over which there have been at least 138 lawsuits, of which less than a dozen have gone to trial.[15] Critics of these practices perceive Monsanto as creating a *chilling effect* in the farming industry, as Monsanto is aware that most farmers do not have the financial resources to invest in legal representation and therefore prematurely settle.

I read about a court that ruled against a farmer who breached an agreement by saving the seeds;[16] another was sentenced to eight months in prison for destroying seeds;[17] yet another farmer was sued because the wind pollinated his land with seeds from a neighboring farm.[18] I also read critiques about seeds not producing the yields as advertised,[19] that the crops are requiring more herbicide,[20, 21, 22] and concerns that genetically modified animal feed may be causing sterility in cattle and pigs.[23] These examples are shared to highlight the strain in your relationship with farmers,[24] leading me to my first question.

Throughout human history, farming was a localized craft intended to empower people to feed themselves. It has since become a prodigious global industry requiring farmers to be chemists and entrepreneurs, politicians and legal scholars. From the reports about your company, it is clear to me that farmers have questions about the science of seeds, they have concerns about business agreements, they have apprehensions about the political process, and they have anxiety about potential litigation. These complexities damage not only your reputation, but also the historic role farmers have played in society.

How will you help restore farmers' dignity by making it a dual priority to reconcile your relationships with them and to encourage farmers to study the environmental impacts of these innovations while openly communicating their findings? In doing this, you would collectively restore credibility to dignified craftsmen historically known for stewardship of the land and whose self-determination and autonomy can benefit everyone.

Relationship with Consumers

My second question is about your relationship with consumers. It is critical for us to understand whether what we ingest preserves health. We have concerns that we may be participating in a system without full awareness of the impacts of our collective decision, not only for our health, but also for the health of animals and the environment.

For example, Canadian, Italian, German, and British studies that found genetically modified crop DNA in the milk, blood, liver, kidneys, and intestinal tissue of animals who were fed genetically modified crops.[25-33] These studies raise concerns that consumers are being exposed to this altered DNA by consuming dairy and meat products. There are also several studies that express concerns about the injection of the growth hormone IGF-1 in cattle who are fed genetically modified crops.[34] It has been argued that when consumed by humans, the milk produced from these cows accelerates the growth of cells in humans, including those associated with breast cancer,[35] prostate cancer,[36] lung cancer, and colon cancers.[37, 38] However, your own studies show that there is no significant difference between milk labeled as "organic milk" and milk without those labels.[39] Our own state Agriculture Secretary, Dennis Wolff, said, "[T]he Pennsylvania Department of Agriculture is not in a position to put warning labels on milk because it would evoke fear in the consumer." Whether or not the labels are there, those of us who read these scientific studies are concerned. Without the ability to fully understand what we are consuming, we make the conjecture that genetically modified crops fed to hormone-injected animals have negative impacts on the health of farm animals and humans. This leads me to ask, simply: How will you support the creation of a system to label all genetically modified foods[40] so that consumers can understand not only how our food is made, but also its impact on our health?

Relationship with the Media

My third question is also about transparency, an ethic your company has publicly pledged to uphold. It is my understanding that one of the goals of your company is to increase productivity in order to feed the world's hungry. However, it is not clearly communicated in the media how much of the food produced is dedicated to those without access to food as compared to how much is grown for animal feed, biofuels, and processed foods in wealthy countries.[41] In other words, consumers are not confident in the authenticity of a slogan that claims to end world hunger. The following example illustrates this same point.

Ten years ago, delegates from the countries of Africa "strongly objected that the image of the poor and hungry from [their] countries" was being used by "giant multinational corporations to push a technology that [they did not consider to be] safe, environmentally friendly, or economically beneficial to [Africans]."[42] They made clear that they did not want to be recipients of genetically modified foods or to have their people be represented in your promotional material; they challenged your company to not mislead consumers.

And yet, last week a French Court sentenced Monsanto for producing a "misleading" commercial that claimed the herbicide Roundup (glyphosate) was "biodegradable" and left "the soil clean." The court said the advertisement, quote, "avoids the potential danger of the product by the use of reassuring words and by misleading the consumer."[43]

This case highlights a chronic strain in your company's relationship with the media, leading me to ask the following question: What will you do to produce truthful advertisements, to encourage reporters to responsibly investigate stories about your products, and to treat all individuals and groups of people with decency and respect? By doing so, you have the opportunity to rebuild public confidence in your company so they may trust your word.

Relationship with Universities

I understand that you have been seeking to rebuild trust with universities, which leads me to ask the fourth question. In February, a group of influential scientists reported to the U.S. Environmental Protection Agency that Monsanto was preventing "university scientists from fully researching the effectiveness and environmental impact of the industry's genetically modified crops." They say they "must seek permission from the seed companies before researching genetically engineered seeds. Sometimes that permission is denied, or the company insists on reviewing any findings before they can be published." One scientist from the University of Minnesota said, "If a company can control the research that appears in the public domain, they can reduce the potential negatives that can come out of any research."[44]

Mr. Grant, the research university plays a unique role in civil society: academic freedom allows researchers to investigate the pressing issues of our time. In doing so, scholars are keepers of an intellectual heritage; they are stewards of our common knowledge, which is betrayed if scholars are legally prevented from producing new knowledge. There is one way Monsanto can transform its image of being a restrictive, closed corporation that seeks to control information: use the open source technology model.

How will you follow the lead of software developers who made their source codes accessible and created a transparent process by which innovations were advanced and profits made? The same can be true of open source biotechnology.[45] Imagine the transformation in your company's image if seed codes were open to peer-based collaboration and public research. We could all partake in the advancement of the science, ensuring that no harm is done to people, animals, or the earth. As the proverb goes, "All of us are smarter than any one of us."

Maybe Monsanto's next innovation will be the production of a *wikiseed*?[46] Imagine an open source code for seeds that invites scientists from around the world into a peer-based collaboration. Such a business strategy would quell concerns about the privatization of the world's seeds. After all, the seed is the origin of the food chain. In this way, the *wikiseed* would allow four freedoms: (1) the freedom for anyone to grow any seed; (2) the freedom to study how the seed works and alter it to achieve different results; (3) the freedom to redistribute seed codes so as to help any world citizen; and (4) the freedom to improve the seed, to release advancements (and modified versions in general) to the public, so that the entire world community benefits. Public access to the genetic code is a precondition to these freedoms. This leads me to ask my fifth question about your relationship with governments.

Relationship with Governments

Just as there are concerns about the privatization of seeds, there are concerns about the politicization of seeds. Citizens of the world are rightfully worried about governments allowing the establishment of an oligopoly—that is, a small number of multinational corporations controlling the world's food supply.[47] This is made possible when companies such as Monsanto hold seed patents in hundreds of countries.

In the U.S. alone, Monsanto and DuPont own nearly all the patents on soy seeds. The patent protects your company for twenty years, thereby ensuring that the seed will eventually become part of the public domain; however, these protections for the public do not take into consideration the practice of a company's replacing one patented seed with another for an indefinite amount of time. For example, a company can distribute to farmers the seeds patented in year one, which is replaced with a new use agreement protecting the seeds licensed in year five, which are soon replaced by new seeds patented in year ten. As a result, the patented seed in year one will become available to the public in year twenty, but farmers will be bound by other use agreements on more advanced seeds. I wonder if this business model establishes a *de facto* breach on patent laws and prevents the most fruitful seeds from being in the public domain.[48]

As a result, there is widespread concern about corporate colonization over what gives life, leading me to ask the fifth question. Mr. Grant, how will Monsanto honor, respect, and protect seed sovereignty, defined as the right of people and self-governed states to democratically determine their own seed policies?[49] By doing so, your company would demonstrate respect for three legacies: self-determination, shared access, and equal opportunity to grown one's own food. The purpose is to simply grant all people the right to plant and reap one's own destiny.

Relationship with Creation

Monsanto's relationship with creation may in fact determine our collective destiny, the subject of my sixth question. During World War II, Monsanto played an important role in the Manhattan Project, which developed the atom bomb,[50] and by the mid-twentieth century Monsanto became one of the top chemical companies in the U.S., eventually producing DDT and Agent Orange used in the Vietnam War to defoliate the environment.[51] Five years ago, your company and Solutia, a spin-off of Monsanto, agreed to a $700 million dollar settlement because of the environmental damage your companies caused when dumping 45 tons of PCB pollutants and mercury into the local creeks of Anniston, Alabama. These toxins not only contaminated the environment, but also the area's drinking water.[52, 53, 54]

Mr. Grant, will you pledge a supermajority of Monsanto's fiscal and human resources to guarantee that our vital ecosystems will never again be contaminated? Will you make a public promise to guarantee to the world citizenry that Monsanto will spend the next century healing, not harming, the environment; healing, not harming, any animals or humans?

Mr. Grant, when can we meet to organize a group of interfaith clergy and bioethicists to craft a twenty-first–century Hippocratic Oath for biotechnology? We could develop an oath based on the principles of biomedical ethics,[55] such as nonmaleficence, beneficence, and justice, to be signed by all Monsanto's employees, affirming their commitment to do no harm.

Relationship with Your Conscience

Before you answer, let your conscience be your guide, for the secret to my seventh question is found in the paradox of my preaching philosophy. I believe that no one listens to my sermons; rather, they take the opportunity to listen to that which is within and beyond. My aim for crafting this sermon as a public letter is to ask you, "Will you take this opportunity to listen to the God of your understanding, to listen to your conscience, and to follow your moral compass?" Monsanto needs a moral leader, not simply for the sake of the company, but for the world community.

My prayer for you is simple: May you hold sacred the responsibility to plant ideas that inspire thoughts, and actions that cultivate not only your character but also our shared destiny.

An ancient parable serves as my closing prayer, dedicated to you: "We pick fruit from trees we did not plant. We draw water from wells we did not dig. This is as it should be, so long as we dig and plant for those who will come after."[56]

Faithfully,

Reverend Nathan C. Walker
First Unitarian Church
2125 Chestnut Street
Philadelphia, PA 19103

APPENDIX F

Ministry with Monsanto

Nathan C. Walker

Preached on July 18, 2010, at the Unitarian Universalist Fellowship of Pottstown, for a joint service with members from the Thomas Paine Unitarian Universalist Fellowship in Collegeville, Pennsylvania. The opening words were offered by Ginni Stiles, Co-Chair of the Ministry Leadership Team of the First Unitarian Church of Philadelphia.

Opening Words

On January 10, 2010, Reverend Nate publicly invited Mr. Grant, the CEO of Monsanto, to meet with a group of interfaith clergy and ethicists to craft a twenty-first–century Hippocratic Oath for the field of biotechnology. The three core principles of the developed oath were derived from biomedical ethics.

First, the term *nonmaleficence* refers to the philosophy of Hippocrates, the father of Western medicine, whose writings call medical professionals to do no harm—meaning: at times it can be wiser to do nothing than do something that may cause more harm than good. The second principle is *beneficence*: the moral obligation to act for the benefit of others. Monsanto has already produced a public statement to this effect. It states, "We will use sound and innovative science and thoughtful and effective stewardship to deliver high-quality products that are *beneficial* to our customers and to the environment." Building upon this pledge, Monsanto has demonstrated the intent to implement a third ethic: *distributive justice*. When applied to the pursuit of doubling the yield of their core crops over the next two decades, Monsanto's goal of "feeding the world's hungry" only becomes feasible through the fair, equitable, and appropriate distribution of food. Reverend Nate stated, "By making the pledge to practice distributive justice, beneficence, and nonmaleficence, Mr. Grant has the opportunity to lead not only his company but the entire field of biotechnology in creating a twenty-first–century oath that can be named after him."

Reverend Nate said, "Imagine the unveiling of the Grant Oath calling those who produce genetically modified foods to consider the possible harm that any pursuit of scientific advancement may have on people, animals, or the environment. Imagine if Mr. Grant were to leave this enduring legacy to humanity, inviting his colleagues to join him in affirming the following pledge:

1. I promise to use my expertise
2. to help and not harm
3. people, animals, and the environment.
4. I promise to practice responsibly
5. the ancient ethic of stewardship
6. and the modern principle of sustainability
7. by affirming distributive justice
8. as a moral obligation
9. to benefit the interdependent web of existence
10. of which we are a part."

The moral invitation to craft such an oath is done with the knowledge that the suffering caused in the past is met with the goodwill offered in the present, that has the potential to influence our collective future. May it be so.

Sermon Introduction

On Thursday night, professionals from Monsanto came to our church for dinner to discuss the ethics of biotechnology. What did we serve? Naturally, we did what churches do best and prepared a potluck. If you were to share a meal with Monsanto, what would you ask and how would you ask your questions?

Members of our church family and representatives from the Unitarian Universalist Association prepared a home-cooked vegetarian meal to offer the same hospitality that Monsanto showed when they responded to my November sermon and invited us to come to St. Louis to meet with the CEO, members of their Board of Directors, executives, and senior scientists.[57] This sermon is designed to summarize the journey that we have taken together in the last nine months—the conception period for our ministry with Monsanto.

Who Is Monsanto?

Those in my parents' generation know Monsanto as a chemical company, which was true for most of the twentieth century, but it has since become a multinational agricultural biotechnology corporation that produces genetically engineered seeds, such as soy, corn, cotton, and now alfalfa. "The market value of the company is $44 billion and last year sold $7.3 billion worth of seeds and seed genes."[58] Less than 10 percent of their research budget is spent on chemicals, and the rest is split evenly between conventional breeding and genetic engineering. On one hand, their conventional research allows for the natural creation of a variety of hybrid seeds that adapt to different soils and weather. On the other hand, their genetic research leads to the discovery of traits found in plants, which is transferred into a seed through a soil bacterium.[59] This can, for example, allow the crop to withstand the herbicide intended to control area weeds so that the crop will produce a higher yield and use less acreage. Monsanto's vision is to "double the yield of their core crops by 2030 through efficient and sustainable means" in order to "meet the food, fiber, and fuel needs of an additional three billion people." Said simply, Monsanto believes it can, in a global system of farmers, governments, and organizations, play one part to help feed the world's hungry.

This mission is not exempt from controversy, as you know. Their work is not free from criticism, nor is it immune from the concerns of the organic industry and consumers. In this context, the purpose of this talk is to summarize the answers we received from employees of Monsanto about a wide range of complex questions that derive from our denominational conversation about ethical eating. I'll do so by surveying the issues at hand; but, first, it is critical to explain the three spiritual practices we brought to our public advocacy.

Spiritual Practices for 21st Century Advocacy

Doubt

The first spiritual practice is doubt. As Unitarian Universalists, we pose questions to one another about our beliefs so that we can reflect upon the authenticity of our words, our deeds. In this way, we are aware that doubt plays a powerful role in our moral and spiritual growth and therefore seek to water the seed that is in all of us. This seed asks a three-word question: "Are you sure? Are you sure?"[60] I've been listening to this seed by asking myself, "Nate, are you sure that your critiques of Monsanto are rooted in the most credible research? Nate, are you sure you are speaking with integrity?" I water this seed of doubt not only to better my character but to model for Monsanto how they can ask, "Are we sure? Are we sure we are doing everything in our power to do no harm, to do good, to be just?" Over the last nine months, members of our church family and employees of Monsanto have found that this seed has guided our dialogue together. We have come to build a relationship based on the mutual commitment to develop a culture of learning established on the second spiritual practice: deep listening and loving speech.

Deep Listening and Loving Speech

We are all aware of the power of words. Language can cause suffering; or, if chosen mindfully and spoken truthfully, can inspire confidence and hope. In this way, we practice compassionate listening and use words that do not demean one another but inspire us to make meaning about complex matters. As you will see in the questions that we've been asking, deep listening and loving speech need not devalue the strength or power of our concerns. This is not a "PC" practice that glosses over reality. It is a way to communicate effectively, to open up conversations rather than use words that lead the listeners to slam their ears shut. Deep listening and loving speech feed our conscience rather than our aggression. We know all too well how fear and anger can plague our thoughts, our words, our actions, leading us to perceive a person, or in this case a company, to be "the other." In those moments, we give ourselves permission to treat "the other" as a stranger to be feared or eliminated. We counter this destructive pattern of "otherizing" with a creative one, based on the third spiritual practice: the imagination.

Imagination

"That which dominates our imaginations and our thoughts will determine our lives, our character" (quote widely attributed to Ralph Waldo Emerson, but may be from someone else).Such wisdom inspires the way Unitarian Universalists engage in global ministry: to develop our moral imagination by picturing ourselves through the eyes of another. This prevents those in the organic community from demonizing the other, [61] treating Monsanto as an organization to be feared. It prevents those in the biotech community from romanticizing the other, treating Monsanto as a company that can never do wrong. In this way, those of us from both the organic and biotech worldviews have engaged this public dialogue by making a covenant based on this simple idea: there is no stranger. We live this ethic by picturing ourselves in another's shoes and thereby intimately weave our imagination with the practice of deep listening and loving speech, and, most importantly, with the spiritual practice of doubt. These ways have been authentically lived out in the last nine months, leading us all to ask simply, "Are any of us really sure?" In that humbling moment, we come to see a larger wisdom, that "all of us are smarter than any one of us."[62]

These spiritual practices were the basis for my direct communication with the CEO of Monsanto. I wrote him a public letter in November in the form of a sermon, which asked Mr. Grant seven moral questions. I will reflect upon the many questions we have explored since then and summarize, to the best of my ability, Monsanto's response. I'll close the talk by casting a vision for our continued ministry together.

Monsanto's Answers to Some of Our Questions

Relationship with Farmers

I asked Monsanto about their relationship with farmers; specifically, why were they investing over $10 million annually for their legal team of seventy-five attorneys?[63] I referenced articles and films that showed interviews with farmers who were sued for breaching technology agreements. They responded by saying that the media has sensationalized the mere dozen or so trials without presenting the big picture. They said that if the public would like to know the quality of their relationship with farmers, they should ask those in the 13 million farms throughout the world that use Monsanto's products, 12 million of which they said are smallholder farms.[64] They explained that it takes seven to fourteen years to roll out a product. Therefore, they have the legal right to seek a return on that investment. They were assured by the courts and various scientific studies that Monsanto's seeds could not have possibly, as critics say, "blown in on the wind" or be "carried by the birds"; rather, the Canadian Supreme Court found one farmer in particular who used Monsanto's patented technology without permission. Monsanto seeks justice about such matters so as to protect the millions of farmers who responsibly honor their use agreements.

Terminator Seeds

They explained that they have not and will never produce "terminator seeds." These are sterile seeds that would not produce offspring seeds for a second season. They want their farmers to succeed and produce more yield. In doing so, they secure long-term clients. In response to the claim that Monsanto seeds are not producing the yields as advertised,[65] a senior scientist at Monsanto stated the studies are inaccurate and are not respected in the scientific community. The proof is found in the fact that "farmers vote one spring at a time. You get invited back if you do a good job," says Mr. Grant. They know they are doing a good job because "ninety percent of the U.S. soybean crop and eighty percent of the corn and cotton crops are grown with seeds containing Monsanto's technology. Other countries are also growing Monsanto's biotech crops, including India, with 20 million acres of cotton; Brazil, with 35 million acres of soybeans; and Argentina, with 43 million acres of soybeans."[66]

Volume of Herbicide and Pesticide Use

When asked about the increased use of herbicides on Monsanto's corn, soybean, and cotton plants, they said the reports used by critics are inaccurate and outdated. They responded by saying that since 1996, farmers who use Monsanto's seeds have seen a significant decrease in pesticide and herbicide use. For example, they state that in the U.S. alone, "Farmers spend more than $3 billion annually on nitrogen fertilizer applications."[67] To counter this practice, they have been developing technology that decreases the use of nitrogen and its runoff into water supplies.

Previous Environmental Damage

I asked about the drinking water in Anniston, Alabama, that was contaminated because forty some years ago, Monsanto dumped 45 tons of PCB pollutants into an open-pit landfill. In 2003, Monsanto and their spin-off company, Solutia, agreed to a $700 million settlement because of this environmental damage. I also asked about their historical involvement in developing DDT and Agent Orange used by the military during the Vietnam War to defoliate the environment. In response to these questions, they explained that Monsanto has since developed a series of pledge statements, one of which says that Monsanto "will use sound and innovative science and thoughtful and effective stewardship to deliver high-quality products that are beneficial to our customers and to the environment."[68] In this way, they spoke of the "old" Monsanto as a chemical company and the "new" Monsanto as the biotech company that aims to feed the world's hungry.

Trust and Sincerity

In multiple ways and at different times during the last nine months, we've asked, "How can we trust the new Monsanto? How can we know these statements are sincere? How do we know these are authentic practices and not simply a public relations response?" The Senior Director of Corporate Responsibility and Sustainable Agriculture replied by saying, "We cannot force you to trust us. Trust is earned. Respect is earned. You'll have to monitor us over time and see whether or not we uphold our pledges. You'll have to see if we respond to stakeholder concerns, and live out our commitment to transparency and dialogue."

In this context, we continued to practice deep listening and loving speech in order to go deeper into the various controversies and competing perceptions about Monsanto.

Effects of GM Foods on Health of Animals and People

We asked them about the international studies that found genetically modified crop DNA in the milk, blood, liver, kidneys, and intestinal tissues of animals who were fed genetically modified (GM) crops.[69] Monsanto scientists explained that these researchers did not go through the peer review process and the findings were not replicated in other studies.[70] And even if they were, the protein IGF-1, which is used as a growth hormone for dairy cows, is naturally found in both animals and humans. They made clear that there is no peer review study that claims this protein is the cause of cancer. They said that "few proteins are known to be toxic" and "very few families of proteins have the potential to induce food allergies when presented in a food matrix."[71]

Monsanto believes that consumers can feel confident in their products because the reviews on Roundup Ready® soybeans, for example, have been completed by over forty regulatory agencies, by regulators in twenty-three countries, and by one region representing the twenty-five member countries of the European Union.[72] If those regulations don't give consumers confidence, they can simply examine current practices. "Estimates suggest that as much as 80% of U.S. processed food may contain an ingredient from a genetically engineered crop, such as corn starch, high-fructose corn syrup, corn oil, canola oil, soybean oil, soy flower, soy lecithin, or cottonseed oil."[73]

Because of the widespread use of GM products, Monsanto feels secure that not only is there an absence of negative effects on the health of animals or people but their products can actually improve our health. For instance, they are currently using the genetic process to identify the omega-3 property found in algae so as to develop a tasteless oil that can not only lower the triglyceride level of people with heart disease but it can help the environment by not depleting fish stock. In this way, they intend to continue funding research that will promote health in people while achieving their pledge of environmental sustainability.

Public Sector Research

When asked about the legitimacy of their studies, we referenced a letter composed by a group of influential scientists who reported to the U.S. Environmental Protection Agency that Monsanto was preventing "university scientists from fully researching the effectiveness and environmental impact of the industry's genetically modified crops." One scientist from the University of Minnesota said, "If a company can control the research that appears in the public domain, they can reduce the potential negatives that can come out of any research."[74] In response to this letter, the American Seed Trade Association gathered these university scientists together to develop a statement that assures Monsanto's commitment to public sector research and encourages them to publish their findings in peer-reviewed scientific or research journals.[75] In this way, Monsanto has made the pledge to "share knowledge and technology to advance scientific understanding, to improve agriculture and the environment, to improve crops, and to help farmers in developing countries."

International Aid

I remember being at a shareholder meeting when another faith-based shareholder, a nun, approached the Director of Human Rights with the idea of sending nongenetically modified hybrid seeds to Haiti. They were both concerned about the devastation from the earthquake and wanted to help farmers have the autonomy to grow their own food. Monsanto then worked with the Haitian Ministry of Agriculture and the U.S. Agency for International Development to donate more than 400 tons of conventional corn seeds. Critics said that Monsanto was going to contaminate the soil and exploit the Haitians for future profit.[76] Monsanto found it ironic that their humanitarian efforts were perceived as causing harm when their previous donations of hybrid seeds to the country of Malawi transformed "a region from a food aid recipient to a food exporter." Monsanto worries that Haiti will do the same thing Zambia did in 2001, when during a famine, the country rejected a cargo of donated corn because they perceived Monsanto's products to be dangerous.[77] Monsanto is aware that people fear what they do not understand and therefore it is Monsanto's goal to help the public understand that biotechnology could solve the world's hunger crisis.

When Worldviews Collide

Put simply, the organic community perceives industrialized biotech efforts as a threat to natural food supplies, biodiversity, and food sovereignty. The biotech community perceives the organic movement to be a threat to environmental sustainability. One of the directors of Monsanto said she stays awake at night worrying that there won't be enough food to feed a growing population. She believes that by using technology to produce more, for less money on less acreage, small farms throughout the world will have access to the resources necessary not only to eat but to earn a living. The organic worldview, however, believes we must eat natural foods, free from chemicals and genetic modification, and that we must eat locally. Monsanto employees think this is a false dualism. Monsanto's mission includes empowering small farmers to succeed so people can eat locally, but they think the organic method is not sustainable nor realistic. They stated, "Organic fields cost $500 per acre to weed by hand, versus only $30 an acre for glyphosate-immune fields." Don Cameron, a cotton farmer in Helm, California, says that he can't even sell organic cotton because the stuff coming out of India, Syria, and Uganda is so cheap. He says, "I feel the organic industry has painted itself in a corner saying that all genetically modified organisms are bad. Eventually they're going to have to allow it," he predicts.[78] In this way, Monsanto hopes that farmers and consumers will have a wide range of organic, hybrid, and genetically engineered options to ensure food security for all. Moreover, they hope more farmers will gain access to the best technology so they can not only produce food for themselves but Monsanto will guarantee the highest ethical standards of the farmers, as noted in their human rights efforts to end child labor.

Human Rights: Child Labor

According to the International Labor Organization, more than 200 million children around the world are used as laborers, and more often than not are involved in the production of agriculture. Monsanto joined leading biotech companies throughout the world to eliminate child labor by requiring farmers to sign contracts that ensure no child will be working the fields, but will instead be attending local schools, partially funded by these companies. In this way, they seek to not only promote human rights but also give farmers from throughout the world the opportunity to produce food.

The Grant Oath

So, when asked whether Monsanto would develop a Hippocratic Oath and vow to "do no harm, to do good, and to be just," they replied uniformly by saying simply, "We already do no harm. We do a lot of good. We are just." They say Monsanto already practices *nonmaleficence,* a term used in the field of biomedical ethics to inspire doctors to "do no harm." Monsanto says that the good caused by biotechnology far outweighs any possible harm to the environment, animals, or people. Monsanto believes it is already practicing *beneficence,* generous acts of doing good, by developing virus-resistant papaya and sweet potatoes in Asia, insect-protected biotech cotton in India, and water-efficient maize in Africa that is expected to create 2 million additional tons of food. They say Monsanto is already upholding the third principle of biomedical ethics by practicing *distributive justice* and promoting the fair, equitable, and appropriate distribution of food.

They are committed to integrating these practices into the culture of Monsanto by requiring all employees to agree upon certain principles, such as never using human or animal DNA-traits in plants. They also require all employees to take a test about their human rights policies, and if they do not receive a score of 100 percent, they are asked to retake the test. These procedures are coupled with their corporate pledges and statements of aspiration based on integrity, dialogue, transparency, sharing, and respect. In this way, Monsanto employees are proud of their company because they see themselves as not only scientists but as philanthropists and humanitarians aligned to feed the world's hungry.

Their sincere communication about these matters leads us to ask the obvious question: if our proposal is to develop a code of ethics for the field of biotechnology, and if Monsanto sees itself as abiding by the proposed ethics, then *why not adopt the oath*?

I have not yet received a formal answer to this question; however, it seems to me like all the right people are meeting at the right time to consider such a request. Together we have been rigorously listening to the seed that asks us, "Are you sure?" We have been consistently practicing deep listening and loving speech so as to not only get at the heart of these complex matters but to also use our moral imagination to picture the world through one another's eyes. These spiritual practices have set the tone for our relationship, which is based on the desire to cultivate mutual respect and understanding, aware that understanding need not imply agreement.

Conclusion

The purpose of this sermon has therefore been to publicly archive the process to date, though we are aware the conversations will continue. We have spent the last nine months conceiving an idea that could potentially give birth to a code of ethics inspiring future generations of biotech professionals. Such an oath would help them feel connected to something larger than themselves, something larger than any company pledge or any norms their worldview permits. We are talking about planting the seed of consciousness in future generations of practitioners, just like many leaders have done in the parallel fields of medicine, law, education, and ministry. But what are the pros and cons of such a code of ethics?

At best, the adoption of such an oath can encourage generations of scientists to speak up about any possible harm their innovations may cause. Imagine if such an oath was in place when the "old" Monsanto operated as a chemical company. The contaminants previously left in the soil call the next generation of scientists to stand on higher ground. Aware that the "new" Monsanto is experiencing a renaissance and leading the relatively new field of biotechnology, we owe it to one another and to future generations to build a global ethic that inspires us all to do no harm.

At worst, such a request could be perceived as a dogmatic proposal from a righteous religious leader who seeks to coerce scientists to adopt his liberal agenda. In this way, it is important for me to recognize that the tone of my initial letter to Mr. Grant was fairly condescending and therefore not effective. I, too, must remember to ask the question, "Are you sure, Nate?" In doing so, the spiritual practice of doubt leads me not to push these particular words but rather to use this draft oath as a conversation starter. Is it possible for us to enter the creative process and redraft an oath that contains more wisdom than any one of us could singularly articulate?

This question makes clear for me the next step we must take. I intend to invite four Monsanto employees to help redraft and then sign the oath. We will then approach a couple professionals at DuPont, then Bayer, and then Syngenta. Once there is a critical mass, we will approach the CEOs of each company and ask for their participation in the creation of another draft. And it's exciting to know that Emmy award-winning filmmaker, Dana Flor, has agreed to document this process by producing a documentary about our ministry with Monsanto.

And, who knows? Maybe someday in the not-so-distant future, universities will confer an oath for future biotechnicians. What will that oath sound like? Only time will tell, but for now, this first draft reads simply,

1. I promise to use my expertise
2. to help and not harm
3. people, animals, and the environment.
4. I promise to practice responsibly
5. the ancient ethic of stewardship
6. and the modern principle of sustainability
7. by affirming distributive justice
8. as a moral obligation
9. to benefit the interdependent web of existence
10. of which we are a part.

Appendix G

Dinner with Monsanto

Michelle Bates Deakin

Published by the UU World *34:4 (Winter 2010)*

A minister is planting the seeds for a code of ethics for bioengineers, starting with Monsanto, the world's largest producer of genetically modified seeds.

On a steamy summer evening in Philadelphia, two senior executives from Monsanto Company walked up the stone steps of the First Unitarian Church of Philadelphia to attend a potluck dinner.

There was classic church supper fare: trays of vegetarian lasagna, bowls of salad, a galvanized tub of iced wine and soda, and chocolate cupcakes lined up in a row. Church members mingled, each with an interest in ethical food production and sustainable agriculture, and all armed with a packet of questions to pose to the executives of Monsanto, the world's largest producer of genetically modified seeds and a leading manufacturer of agricultural chemicals.

It was an unusual combination of dinner guests: nine Unitarian Universalists in casual summer dress and two polished corporate spokeswomen in tailored suits and pearls. The Rev. Nate Walker floated among them, with a wide smile and welcoming hugs, making introductions.

Since November 2009, Walker has been engaged in an unlikely ministry. This minister of a 220-member urban Unitarian Universalist church has cultivated a public dialogue with the $44 billion multinational public corporation, posing complex ethical questions and listening carefully as the company answers.

At Monsanto's invitation, he flew to the company's St. Louis headquarters, toured its facilities, and met with executives and scientists. He attended Monsanto's annual meeting and has brainstormed about ethical food production with religious leaders from the Interfaith Center on Corporate Responsibility. And with this dinner, the conversation was expanding to include his congregation.

Walker's goal is to inspire Monsanto to adopt a sort of Hippocratic Oath, akin to a doctor's pledge to "do no harm." Ultimately, he'd like executives from DuPont, Bayer, and Syngenta, the nation's other leading producers of bioengineered seed, to sign the oath, too. The oath is a two-sentence, fifty-three-word pledge to protect people and the environment. The language will be familiar to any Unitarian Universalist, echoing the Unitarian Universalist Association's Seventh Principle. It reads:

> I promise to use my expertise to help and not harm people, animals, and the environment. I promise to practice responsibly the ancient ethic of stewardship and the modern principle of sustainability by affirming distributive justice as a moral obligation to benefit the interdependent web of existence of which we are a part.

As the dinner guests gathered, Walker's blue eyes gleamed with anticipation. For months, he had been planning the occasion at which congregants and Monsanto executives would break bread together, talk, and listen to one another. "This conversation is the best of Unitarian Universalism, where we each out of consciousness develop our perspectives," he said. "A minister dreams to see so many thoughtful people in a room engaged in the moral issues of our time."

One year ago, on November 1, 2009, Walker preached a sermon about Monsanto's corporate practices that drew the attention of environmental activists, scientists, and, somewhat to Walker's surprise, of Monsanto itself.

The sermon sprouted from Walker's preparations to teach a class at his church on ethical eating. Like many congregations, First Unitarian is exploring how individual food choices affect local communities and the greater world, following the UUA General Assembly's decision in 2008 to adopt "ethical eating" as a Congregational Study / Action Issue for four years.

Walker wrote his sermon, called "Sovereign Seeds," as an open letter to Hugh Grant, Monsanto's chairman, president, and CEO. In the sermon, Walker challenged Grant to respond to seven "moral questions" about Monsanto's relationships with farmers, consumers, media, academic scientists, governments, and creation, and about Grant's relationship with his own conscience. Walker's questions reflected many progressives' and environmentalists' critiques of Monsanto's practices.

Walker hoped that the sermon would plant a seed that, he wrote, "if grown collectively, can heal some of the most critical relationships of our time."

Walker expressed concerns about Monsanto's "strained" relationships with farmers, who have come to depend on Monsanto's genetically modified herbicide-resistant seeds, but who have sometimes bristled at the company's restrictive licenses or expressed concerns about the side-effects of genetic engineering. "From the reporting about your company," Walker said, "it is clear to me that farmers have questions about the science of seeds, they have concerns about business agreements, they have apprehensions about the political process, and they have anxiety about potential litigation. These complexities damage not only your reputation but also the historic role farmers have played in society." He asked how Monsanto would repair these relationships.

With regard to consumers, Walker's sermon posed this question: "How will you support the creation of a system to label all genetically modified foods so that consumers can understand not only how our food is made but also its impact on our health?"

He asked how the company would make itself more transparent with the media. He asked how it will improve its relationships with governments, who worry that Monsanto and a small number of multinational corporations are coming to control the world's seed supply. He asked about its relationship with universities, whose scientists have complained that Monsanto will not allow them to research the effectiveness and environmental impact of its genetically modified crops. Walker suggested Monsanto follow the lead of software developers who make their source codes accessible. "Imagine the transformation in your company's image if seed-codes were open to peer-based collaboration and public research," he said.

Walker questioned Monsanto's impact on the environment in the past, including its role in the Manhattan Project, which developed the atom bomb; its part in developing DDT and Agent Orange; and its degradation of the environment in sites such as Anniston, Alabama, where the company dumped PCBs and mercury into creeks and agreed to a $700 million settlement with residents. "Will you make a public promise to guarantee the world's citizenry that Monsanto will spend the next century healing, not harming, the environment; healing, not harming, animals and humans?" Walker asked Grant. (Starting in 1997, Monsanto sold off the divisions involved in these projects to concentrate on agricultural chemicals and seeds.) And further, Walker challenged Grant to take an oath based on the principles of biomedical ethics.

Lastly, Walker asked the CEO, "Will you take this opportunity to listen to the God of your understanding, to listen to your conscience, and to follow your moral compass? Monsanto needs a moral leader, not simply for the sake of the company but for the world community."

The next day, Walker express-mailed a copy of the sermon to Grant, and uploaded the text and a podcast of the sermon to the church website and his personal website. For a month, he heard nothing from the corporation. But responses from around the country began to pour in. He received letters from Michael Pollan, author of *In Defense of Food* and *The Omnivore's Dilemma*, popular books that explore where today's food comes from and its effect on people and the environment, and from Robert Kenner, director of the movie *Food, Inc.,* a documentary that examines how the nation's food supply is controlled by a handful of corporations. Walker also received letters from scientists and activists at the Union of Concerned Scientists, the Center for Food Safety, and the Midwest Coalition for Responsible Investment.

Then a letter from Monsanto arrived. It was from Diane B. Herndon, the senior director of corporate responsibility and sustainable agriculture, and it included an invitation to come to the company's headquarters in St. Louis. Herndon and Maureen Mazurek, Monsanto's director of human rights, were the company spokespeople who eventually came to Philadelphia.

Both Monsanto executives described Walker's sermon as thoughtful. They watched his sermon on YouTube and found him "passionate." "His sermon was earnest and respectful," said Herndon. "And all of the things he suggested were things we were thinking about. We thought, 'He probably doesn't realize all that is taking place at Monsanto.'"

Mazurek added, "We felt like Rev. Nate was a key influence leader, but we felt he only had part of the story. We wanted to give him an opportunity to learn by inviting him here."

Herndon, Mazurek, and Walker began planning Walker's January 2010 trip to St. Louis. Though Herndon and Mazurek had watched him on YouTube, read his words, and spoken to him on the phone, they were still surprised by the man who showed up.

Walker's words are forceful, but he is a gentle man who listens more than he talks, his eyes focused intently on the speaker, his hands still. A vegetarian since he was a child, Walker, 34, is trim, with close-cropped sandy blond hair. He grew up on an alfalfa farm in Nevada. A naturalist and an intellectual, Walker is pursuing an interdisciplinary doctorate in law, education, and religion at Columbia University.

"I've been with Monsanto for eighteen years, and people come here with their own agenda, not with their listening ears," said Mazurek. "He came in a genuine way, with a willingness to share and have a dialogue."

Walker said that he is not interested in "demeaning people." Rather, he seeks to "make meaning." He said he is guided by the practices of deep listening and loving speech. And he is inspired by the words of Zen master Thich Nhat Hahn, who speaks of planting seeds of consciousness by always asking oneself the question: "Are you sure?" Walker even shared this spiritual practice with Monsanto executives. "It was a meaningful conversation," he said.

In St. Louis, he met with executives and scientists. Monsanto executives also invited him to attend a shareholders' meeting as a guest, where Walker was briefly introduced to Grant, the CEO. Walker's church is not a direct shareholder in Monsanto. First Unitarian's endowment, however, does hold investments in mutual funds that include Monsanto stock. Walker listened to Monsanto executives and to shareholders, including members of the Interfaith Center for Corporate Responsibility, which buys stock in public corporations so that it can influence policy through shareholder resolutions and by speaking directly with corporate management.

Walker, Mazurek, and Herndon agreed that the next step would be for Monsanto to continue the dialogue they had started with Walker's parishioners in Philadelphia. They set the date for July.

Monsanto would not allow a reporter to attend the dinner. "We were [are] committed to continuing the dialogue with [Walker] and his congregation, but not opening it up to the point where it could become a 'media event,'" Herndon wrote in an e-mail. Herndon and Mazurek spoke with *UU World* before and after the dinner, but the dinner conversation itself was closed.

When the doors to the Parish Room opened after the dinner, an air of goodwill prevailed. Members described the meeting as "a learning process." Anne Slater, secretary of the church's board, said she was interested to hear the high standards that the company sets for itself. Another wondered why the company didn't publish a magazine to tell the public about its good deeds, such as donating $4 million worth of conventional corn and vegetable seed to Haiti after the devastating earthquake in January 2010. Members described Monsanto's commitment to increasing world food production for a growing population and how it was guided by its "Monsanto Pledge."

Herndon described the meeting as "thoughtful, sincere, and constructive." Walker said, "I feel really moved."

The following morning, Walker held a meeting in his upstairs office with two church members who had attended the dinner, Ginni Stiles, co-chair with Walker of the church's ministry leadership team, and Luana Goodwin, president of the church's board of trustees, along with Rowan Van Ness, environmental justice program associate at the Unitarian Universalist Ministry for the Earth. Each reflected on the dinner and what the church's next steps should be.

They responded positively to the dinner and the dialogue, but as they picked the meeting apart, areas for further discussion arose. Stiles was concerned that the congregants' questions reflected philosophical ideas, while Monsanto "delivered corporation communication-type sentences."

Van Ness said she was struck by Mazurek's confession that what keeps her up at night are concerns about people who champion strictly organic food; the organic agenda, Mazurek had said, was not sustainable for a growing world population. (Van Ness wrote about her reactions to the conversation on the UUA's "Inspired Faith, Effective Action" blog, July 20, 2010.)

Goodwin expressed uneasiness about pushing Monsanto to sign the oath Walker had drafted. "I have a problem with the oath concept. I see it as religion and telling people to express themselves in the way that we have found to express ourselves," she said. "It's the conversation that is important, not the end point." Goodwin said she and the board of trustees would discuss becoming a direct investor in Monsanto so that the church could gain shareholder rights.

The Interfaith Center on Corporate Responsibility has been raising concerns with Monsanto as a shareholder for decades, both to change company policy and to educate other shareholders about environment, health, and patent issues. "Faith communities can have an influence," said Margaret Weber, a board member of ICCR and corporate responsibility director for the Congregation of St. Basil, an international order of Catholic priests. "Nate's sermon and letter are very significant," she said. Although groups such as ICCR and its local affiliate, the Midwest Coalition for Responsible Investing, have been active in shareholder discussions, Weber said that, "in the pews, it's been pretty quiet on this issue. Nate's public letter and his whole approach about doing no harm has been powerful."

Monsanto's "Pledge" contains seven policy commitments about how Monsanto will do business. The company's corporate responsibility and sustainability report describes it as "a declaration that compels us to listen more, to consider our actions and their impact broadly, and to lead responsibly." Herndon and Mazurek both say that it supplants any need for the oath that Walker has proposed.

Walker, however, sees the oath he is promoting as an important step toward developing a code of ethics for the field of biotechnology. "We have spent the last nine months conceiving an idea that could potentially give birth to a code of ethics that could inspire future generations of biotech professionals. Such an oath could help them feel connected to something larger than themselves, something larger than any company pledge, or any norms their worldview permits," said Walker, in a sermon to the Thomas Paine Unitarian Universalist Fellowship in Collegeville, Pennsylvania, where he preached the Sunday after the July Monsanto dinner. "We're talking about planting the seeds of consciousness in future generations of practitioners."

Walker said he is inviting Herndon and Mazurek to help him redraft the oath so that they feel comfortable signing it and recommending that other Monsanto executives sign it, too. Nine months after their initial conversations began, Herndon wrote Walker to tell him that an industry association, CropLife International, has a voluntary Plant Biotechnology Code of Conduct for members, and that Walker should work directly with that trade group instead. Herndon, however, was laid off in October.

Walker plans to approach executives at other agriculture biotechnology companies and ask them to help further hone an oath. And he envisions enlisting universities as well, so that students graduating with degrees in biotechnology can take a pledge to do no harm as they begin their professions. Walker also wants to inspire biotech companies to hire ethicists or ombudsmen who could hold a mirror up to their companies and continually ask whether company practices are in line with the ethical oath.

One day, anyone may be able to watch how it all unfolds. Walker is working with Dana Flor, an Emmy Award-winning filmmaker who is going to document the process of Walker working with the executives. The working title for the documentary is *Sacred Seeds*. Flor is preparing a summary of the film to pitch to outlets such as HBO and the Discovery Channel.

Throughout the process, Walker pledges to continue to listen to his own sacred seed, which asks him, "Are you sure?"

Update: August 2014

Since the publication of the *UU World* article, the executives at Monsanto have declined to redraft or sign the oath because they believe they already "do no harm." The proposed documentary has been put on hold because of a conflict of interest: Dana Flor is related to an employee of Monsanto's competitor DuPont. Reverend Nate has also recommended that the Unitarian Universalist Association either partner with the Interfaith Center on Corporate Responsibility and engage in regular and sustained shareholder advocacy with the biotech industry or divest from these companies, just as the delegates at the July 2014 General Assembly of Unitarian Universalist Associations affirmed the fossil fuel divestment resolution.

Notes

[1] Martin Luther King, Jr. (1967) "A Time to Break Silence," delivered at Riverside Church in New York, New York on April 4, 1967.

[2] "A Kol Nidrei," in Mark Bellitini, *Sonata for Voice and Silence: Meditations* (Boston: Skinner House Press, 2011), 22–23. Reprinted with permission.

[3] "Education Level by Religious Tradition" in *U.S. Religious Landscape Survey,* Pew Forum on Religion and Public Life, Washington D.C. (Accessed at http:// religions.pewforum.org/pdf/table-education-by-tradition.pdf)

[4] *Rumi and his Sufi Path of Love* (2007) Fatih Citlak and Huseyin Bingul (Somerset, New Jersey: Tughra Books), 81

[5] I consider this opening statement to mean that *most* or *many* religious, ethical, and spiritual traditions promote the principle of compassion.

[6] For an explanation of the term "return to the ancient principle," see how Karen Armstrong emphasizes the hermeneutical practices of Augustine (353–430) and others in "The First Step: Learn about Compassion," in *Twelve Steps to a Compassionate Life* (New York: Alfred A. Knopf, 2010), 25–64.

[7] Phyllis Trible, *Texts of Terror* (Philadelphia: Fortress Press, 1984), 1.

[8] Often attributed to John Murray (1741–1815), this quote derives from Alfred S. Cole, *Our Liberal Heritage* (Boston: Beacon Press, 1951). For a detailed discussion see Peter Huges, "Who Really Said That?" *UU World,* November 15, 2012.

[9] Sheryl Prenzlau, *The Jewish Children's Bible: Exodus,* illustrated by Zely Smekhov and Lena Guberman (New York: Pitspopany Press, 1997).

[10] "It Matters What We Believe," Sophia Lyon Fahs, reading #657 in *Singing the Living Tradition.* (Boston: Unitarian Universalist Association, 1993.)

[11] Malcolm X and Alex Haley, *The Autobiography of Malcolm X: As Told to Alex Haley* (1973; orig. New York: Ballantine, 1964), 201–2.

[12] "Section C-2.1. Principles," *Unitarian Universalist Association Bylaws and Rules* (Boston: Unitarian Universalist Association, as amended through July 1, 2014).

[13] Marie-Monique Robin. Documentary: *The World According to Monsanto,* 11 March 2008. (http://www.youtube.com/watch?v=swVjzIVqRUA). Retrieved 30 October 2009. The complete film is posted at (http://video.google.com/videopla y?docid=6262083407501596844#).

[14] *Third World Network Biosafety Information Service,* 20 January 2005. (http:// www.twnside.org.sg/title2/service155.htm). Retrieved 30 October 2009.

[15] According to www.monsanto.com, there have been "138 lawsuits, with less than a dozen having gone to trial." Retrieved 30 October 2009.

[16] *Monsanto Company v. McFarling* (2007). (http://bit.ly/22qpeS). Retrieved 31 October 30 2009.

[17] Peter Shinkle, "Farmer who lied in dispute with Monsanto will go to prison," *St. Louis Post-Dispatch,* 7 May 2003. (http://www.gene.ch/genet/2003/ May/msg00044.html). Retrieved 30 October 2009.

[18] *Monsanto Canada Inc. v. Schmeiser* (2004). 1 S.C.R. 902, 2004 SCC 34.

[19] See Doug Gurian-Sherman, *Failure to Yield: Evaluating the Performance of Genetically Engineered Crops,* Union of Concerned Scientists (April 2009). For a critique of this publication, see *PG Economics Limited* briefing note: 17 April 2009. Also see Geoffrey Lean, "Exposed: The Great GM Myth," in *The Independent,* 20 April 2008. Please note Dr. Barney Gordon's rebuttal: "Manganese Nutrition of

Glyphosate-Resistant and Conventional Soybeans… Setting the Record Straight," in *Better Crops*, 28 April 2008.

[20]An international peer-review journal published an article by eight international experts from three continents claiming that agricultural GMO developers and regulatory agencies have systematically neglected secondary effects of GMOs and pesticides and calling for "more serious standardized tests such as those used for pesticides or drugs, on at least three mammalian species tested for at least three months employing larger sample sizes, and up to one and two years before commercialization, for GM food or feed specifically modified to contain pesticide residues. We also call for a serious scientific debate about the criteria for testing significant adverse health effects for pesticides or chemicals, but overall for GM food or feed products, such as MON 863." Séralini, Gilles-Eric, et al., "How Subchronic and Chronic Health Effects Can be Neglected for GMOs, Pesticides or Chemicals," *International Journal of Biological Sciences* (2009): 5:438–43, Ivyspring International Publisher.

[21]"Genetically engineered corn, soybeans, and cotton have led to a 122 million pound increase in pesticide use since 1996. While Bt crops have reduced insecticide use by about 15.6 million pounds over this period, HT [herbicide tolerant] crops have increased herbicide use 138 million pounds." "One study of more than 8,000 university-based field trials suggested that farmers who plant Roundup Ready soy use two to five times more herbicide than non-GE farmers who use integrated weed-control methods." Visit (http://bit.ly/1eWXM) as referenced in Charles Benbrook, "Evidence of the Magnitude of the Roundup Ready Soybean Yield Drag from University-Based Varietal Trials in 1988," *Agricultural Biotechnology InfoNet Technical Paper* Number 1, July 13, 1999. (http://www.mindfully.org/GE/RRS-Yield-Drag.htm). Retrieved 30 October 2009.

[22]"Who Benefits from GM Crops? Feeding the Biotech Giants, Not the World's Poor," *Friends of the Earth International*, issue 116 (February 2009).

[23]See the interviews with farmers in the documentary *Patent for a Pig* at (http://video.google.com/videoplay?docid=1669587865067156619&hl=en#). Retrieved 30 October 2009. Please note, in 2007, Monsanto sold Monsanto Choice Genetics to Newsham Genetics LC of West De Moines, Iowa. Monsanto's rebuttal to this documentary and to Greenpeace, who also claimed Monsanto was patenting pig genes, was as follows, "When Monsanto owned the business, the company performed research work for a patent application related to a specific gene marker for a pig trait, but not for the trait itself, and also a patent application for a unique set of breeding processes, including an artificial insemination method. Monsanto never filed a patent application for a pig gene." Updated 16 July 2009 at (http://www.monsanto.com/monsanto_today/for_the_record/pig_patent.asp).

[24]For a counter argument to the premise of my position, please watch the videos *Farmer Choice* at (http://www.youtube.com/watch?v=F7Ne_uqqscQ) and *Family Farmers* at (http://www.youtube.com/watch?v=Mn8qHLh3SX0), and the public statements published at (http://www.monsanto.com/foodinc/monsanto_monopoly.asp) and *Celebrating the American Farmer* at (http://www.monsanto.com/americanfarmer/default.asp?WT.svl=1). All retrieved 30 October 2009.

[25]R.H. Phipps, E.R. Deaville, and B.C. Maddison, "Detection of transgenic and endogenous plant DNA in rumen fluid, duodenal digesta, milk, blood, and feces of lactating dairy cows," *Journal of Dairy Sci*ence, vol. 86, (2003):4070–78.

[26]E.H. Chowdhury, et al., "Fate of maize intrinsic and recombinant genes in calves fed genetically modified maize Bt11," *Journal of Food Protection*, vol. 67 (2004): 365–70.

[27]R. Einspanier, et al., "The fate of forage plant DNA in farm animals: a collaborative case study investigating cattle and chicken fed recombinant plant material," *European Food Research and Technology*, vol. 212 (2001): 129–34.

[28]R.H. Phipps, D.E. Beever, and D.J. Humphries, "Detection of transgenic DNA in milk from cows receiving herbicide tolerant (CP4EPSPS) soybean meal," *Livestock Production Science*, vol. 74 (2002): 269–73.

[29]R. Sharma, et al., "Detection of Transgenic and Endogenous Plant DNA in Digesta and Tissues of Sheep and Pigs Fed Roundup Ready Canola Meal," *Journal of Agricultural and Food Chemistry* vol. 54 (2006: 1699–1709.

[30]R. Mazza, et al., "Assessing the transfer of genetically modified DNA from feed to animal tissues," *Transgenic Research,* vol. 14 (2005): 775–84.

[31]A. Agodi, et al., "Detection of genetically modified DNA sequences in milk from the Italian market," *International Journal of Hygiene and Environmental Health*, vol. 209 (2006): 81–88.

[32]"Submission: Senate Select Committee on Agricultural and Related Industries," retrieved at (http://bit.ly/1oRi2P) on 30 October 2009.

[33]Ralf Einspanier, *Report on examination to determine plant and Bt-maize residues in cow milk*, conducted at the Weihenstephan research centre for milk and foodstuffs of the Technical University of Munich-Freising, 20 October 2000 and 20 December 2000.

[34]It was stated that investigative reporters Steve Wilson and Jane Akre "were fired from Fox News" before broadcasting information about Monsanto's growth hormone, as noted in "Fox News Kills Monsanto Milk Story" (http://www.youtube.com/watch?v=axU9ngbTxKw) and in the documentary *The Corporation* (http://www.youtube.com/watch?v=eZkDikRLQrw). Retrieved 30 October 2009.

[35]"High circulating IGF-I concentrations would be associated with an increased risk of breast cancer," as noted in S.E. Hankinson, et al., "Circulating concentrations of insulin-like growth factor-I and risk of breast cancer," *The Lancet*, vol. 351, no. 9113 (1998): 1393–96.

[36]"Results raise concern that administration of GH or IGF-I over long periods, as proposed for elderly men to delay the effects of aging (34), may increase risk of prostate cancer," as noted in J.M. Chan, et al., "Plasma insulin-like growth factor-I and prostate cancer risk: a prospective study," *Science*, vol. 279, no. 5350 (1998): 563–66.

[37]"This review summarizes key results in this field and provides a hypothesis concerning the mechanism by which IGF physiology influences risk of common epithelial cancers including those of breast, prostate, lung and colon," as noted in M. Pollak, "Insulin-like growth factor physiology and cancer risk," *European Journal of Cancer*, 36, 10 (June 2000): 1224–28.

[38]"The increased IGF-I bioavailability may, over time, increase the risk of colorectal cancer," as noted in M.S. Sandhu, D.B. Dunger, and E.L. Giovannucci, "Insulin, insulin-like growth factor-I (IGF-I), IGF binding proteins, their biologic interactions, and colorectal cancer," *Journal of the National Cancer Institute*, 94, 13(2002): 972–80.

[39]J. Vicini, T. Etherton, et al., "Survey of retail milk composition as affected by label claims regarding farm-management practices." *Journal of the American Dietetic Association*, 108, 7 (2008): 1198–203.

[40]David Barboza, "Modified Foods Put Companies in a Quandary," *The New York Times*, 4 June 2000.

[41]"Who Benefits from GM Crops?" *Friends of the Earth International.* "Friends of the Earth International is the world's largest grassroots environmental network, uniting 77 diverse national member groups and some 5,000 local activist groups on every continent. With approximately 2 million members and supporters around the world, we campaign on today's most urgent social and environmental issues."

[42]"Let Nature's Harvest Continue," statement from all the African delegates (except South Africa) to FAO negotiations on the International Undertaking for Plant Genetic Resources, 5th Extraordinary Session of the Commission on Genetic Resources, 8–12 June 1998, Rome.

[43]R. Boughriet, "La 'Montre Verte' mesure les niveaux de bruit et d'ozone en milieu urbain," 19 October 2009 (http://www.actu-environnement.com/ae/news/fing_ile_de_france_montre_verte_sfr_morizet_futur_en_ seine_7500.php4). Retrieved 30 October 2009.

[44]Andrew Pollack, "Crop Scientists Say Biotechnology Seed Companies Are Thwarting Research," *The New York Times*, February 20, 2009.

[45]S.M. Maurer, "Open source biology: Finding a niche (or maybe several)," *UMKC Law Review* 76, 2 (2008).

[46]I independently thought of this term; however, I later discovered that there are websites that use this word but do not have the same meaning.

[47]Erosion, Technology and Concentration Action Group, *Communiqué,* issue 90 (September/October 2005).

[48]Equally disconcerting is the practice of Monsanto former employees currently holding positions in the U.S. agencies, for example the Food and Drug Administration and the Environmental Protection Agency. This also applies to U.S. Supreme Court Justice Clarence Thomas.

[49]Food Sovereignty is defined in the "Global Report: Agriculture at a Crossroads" (2009) by the International Assessment of Agricultural Knowledge Science and Technology for Development (IAASTD) as "the right of peoples and sovereign states to democratically determine their own agricultural and food policies." Food Security "exists when all people of a given spatial unit, at all times, have physical and economic access to sufficient, safe, and nutritious food to meet their dietary needs and food preferences for an active and healthy life and that such food is obtained in a socially acceptable and ecologically sustainable manner."

[50]See "Monsanto's Greatest Hits" (http://www.metroactive.com/papers/metro/05.11.00/cover/gen-food2-0019.html).

[51]Rachel Carson, *Silent Spring* (Boston: Houghton Mifflin, 1962).

[52]Michael Grunwald, "Monsanto Hid Decades of Pollution: PCBs Drenched Ala. Town, but No One Was Ever Told," *Washington Post,* Page A01, 1 January 2002.

[53]Kevin Sack, "PCB Pollution Suits Have Day in Court in Alabama." *The New York Times,* 27 January 2002.

[54]AP Staff Writer, "$700 million deal announced in Anniston PCBs cases." *Associated Press,* 19 August 2003.

[55]Tom Beauchamp and James F. Childress, *Principles of Biomedical Ethics* (New York: Oxford University Press, 1979).

[56]Unknown source.

[57]We met or talked with Dr. Natalie DiNicola, Director, Global Development Partnership; Kevin Eblen, Vice President, Public Policy & Sustainable Yield; Dr. Leigh English (Unitarian Universalist), Director of Research Centre, Bangalore, India; Janice L. Fields, Board of Directors, Chief Operating Officer of McDonald's; Dr. Dan Goldstein, Senior Science Fellow; Mr. Hugh Grant, Chief Executive Officer; Gwendolyn S. King, Board of Directors; Thomas Helscher, Director, Public Affairs; Diane Herndon, Director, Corporate Responsibility and Sustainable Yield; Maureen Mazurek, Director, Human Rights, Stakeholder Engagement; Dr. Jim Mieure, tour guide at the Chesterfield Village research facility; Dr. Eric Sachs, Director, Global Scientific Affairs; Nancy Vosnidou (Unitarian Universalist), Lead, Patent Science Group; and Glynn Young, Director, Environmental Communications.

[58]Robert Langreth and Matthew Herper, "Company of the Year: The Planet Versus Monsanto: Monsanto's first round of attackers said its seeds were evil. Now the charge is that Monsanto's seeds are too good," *Forbes Magazine,* January 18, 2010.

[59]Agrobacterium tumefaciens.

[60]Thich Nhat Hahn, a Vietnamese Zen Master, taught Reverend Nate about this seed of mindfulness at a meditation retreat that took place from October 2–6, 2010, at Blue Mountain Mediation Center in New York.

[61]Robert Schreiter, *The Ministry of Reconciliation: Spirituality and Strategies* (Maryknoll, New York: Orbis Books), 63–64.

[62]A Japanese proverb.

[63]Lim Li Lin and Chee Yoke Heong, "Dear Friends and Colleagues, RE: Monsanto v. US Farmers," Open Letter by the Third World Network Biosafety Information Service, 20 January 2005. (http://www.twnside.org.sg/title2/service155.htm). Retrieved 30 October 2009.

[64]In January, Monsanto professionals verbally shared this information, but there still needs to be a fact-check and a specific definition of "smallholder farms."

[65]See the 2009 study by the Union of Concerned Scientists that calculated that "only 14% of recent corn-crop yield increases are due to genetically engineered Bt corn. Roundup ready corn and soy seeds don't increase crop yield at all, it found." Quoted in Robert Langreth and Matthew Herper, "Company of the Year: The Planet Versus Monsanto: Monsanto's first round of attackers said its seeds were evil. Now the charge is that Monsanto's seeds are too good," *Forbes Magazine,* January 18, 2010.

[66]Lagreth and Herper, "Company of the Year."

[67]See "Monsanto and Evogene Collaborate on Nitrogen Use Efficiency Research," News Release, September 25, 2007 at 9:00 a.m. (http://monsanto.mediaroom.com/index.php?s=43&item=534&printable).

[68]See *Benefits* in the "The Monsanto Pledge" as published at (http://www.monsanto.com/who_we_are/our_pledge/monsanto_pledge.asp).

[69]For complete citations see my November 1, 2009, sermon entitled *Sovereign Seeds*, endnotes 13-21.

[70]For a full critique of the studies see "For the Record – Science: Monsanto Response: de Vendomois et al. 2009. *A Comparison of the Effects of Three GM Corn Varieties on Mammalian Health.* 'Assessment of quality and response to technical issues'" as published by Monsanto Scientific Affairs, September 2009.

[71]J. Jenkins, S. Griffiths-Jones, P. Shewry, H. Breitender, and E. Mills, "Structural Relatedness of Plant Food Allergens with Specific References to Cross-Reactive," *Journal of Allergy and Clinical Immunology,* 115 (2005): 163–70.

[72]In addition, the October 2000 recall of food products containing Starling™ later concluded that the "Bt protein was not involved in the allergic reactions of the 17 individuals tested. But uncertainty still exists because blood and food samples were not received form all 28 individuals who experienced a true allergic reaction." See page 787 of Peggy G. Lemaux, "Genetically Engineered Plants and Foods: A Scientist's Analysis of the Issues (Part I)," *Annual Review of Plant Biology* 59 (2008):771-812.

[73]W.K. Hallman, W.C. Hebden, H.L. Aquino, C.L. Cutie, and J.T. Lang, "Public Perceptions of Genetically Modified Foods: A National Study of American Knowledge and Opinion," *International Food Policy Institute* (2003): 1003–1004. New Brunswick, N.J.: Rutgers Univiversity. Quoted in Peggy G. Lemaux, (2008). "Genetically Engineered Plants and Foods: A Scientist's Analysis of the Issues (Part I), *Annual Review of Plant Biology* 59 (2008):771-812

[74]Pollack, Andrew, "Crop Scientists Say Biotechnology Seed Companies are Thwarting Research," *The New York Times,* 20 February 2009.

[75]See *Research with Commercially Available Seed Products,* as prepared by the American Seed Trade Association, Approved September 17, 2009, Final.

[76]For example, see Ronnie Cummins' article, "Monsanto's Poison Pills for Haiti," published in the *Huffington Post* on May 24, 2010. Cummins is the Founder and Director of the Organic Consumers Association and said, "Hybrid seeds, like GMO seeds (in contrast to Creole heirloom or organic seeds) require lots of water, chemical fertilizers, and pesticides. In addition, if a small farmer tries to save hybrid seeds after harvest, hybrid seeds usually do not 'breed true' or grow very well in the second season, forcing the now-indentured peasant to buy seeds from Monsanto or one of the other hybrid/GMO seed monopolies in perpetuity."

[77]*Famine-hit Zambia rejects GM food aid,* BBC News, World Edition, Tuesday, 29 October, 2002, 18:25 GMT as retrieved at (http://news.bbc.co.uk/2/hi/africa/2371675.stm).

[78]Lagreth and Herper, "Company of the Year," 67.